MW00637803

I'mPatiently
Impatient

Improbable Adventures of an
Entrepreneur with ADHD

This item is no longer property
of Sun City Oro Valley Library
Sale of this item benefited the Library

LARRY BROPHY

A TRUE STORY

DISCARD
SunCity
ORO VALLEY
OCT 1565 E. Rancho Vistoso Blvd.
Oro Valley, AZ 85755

I'mPatiently Impatient
Copyright © 2020 by Larry Brophy. All rights reserved.

No part of this publication may be reproduced, stored in a retrieval system or transmitted in any way by any means, electronic, mechanical, photocopy, recording or otherwise without the prior permission of the author except as provided by USA copyright law.

Published in the United States of America

L&L Marketing, LLC
1001 S. Main Street, Suite 49
Kalispell, MT 59901

ISBN: 978-0-578-73839-0

Contents

Preface

This is a true story. All of the people, places, dates and events are accurately recorded. I trust anyone mentioned in this book will appreciate the role that they've played in my life.

Attention Deficit Hyperactivity Disorder, or ADHD wasn't well known outside of the medical community until the 1980's. Although I've never been clinically diagnosed with this condition, my life is a testament to its effects throughout life.

What follows is the saga of my life journey. It's a story of constant change and pushing myself out of my comfort zone. It's written in active, first person so you may experience it along with me.

This story is full of numerous adventures; of repeated failures and occasional successes; of crushing disappointment and devastating despair, as well as unbridled happiness and intense ecstasy.

Welcome to my life.

Introduction

THE STORY

Each of us has a story
and each one is different...
except the beginning
and the absolute end

Everything in the middle

Is unique to each of us, for
it's the story of our life

We're the author of our own story
We can put in –
or leave out
whatever we desire
We ourselves limit our desires
for whatever we desire
strongly enough
cannot help but become our story

One day each of us will have
our own story read
for it can only be read
as it was written

What will be your feeling
when your personal story is read?

Does the thought bring excitement –
deep feelings of dread –
or worse, regret?

We write our own story one day at a time
and alone have the power
to make the words dissonant
or to make the words rhyme

This is my story.

1 | Polio

I sit on the edge of my bunkbed and the doctor tells me to look at my belly button. I try. No matter how hard I try, I can't seem to bend my head down. He tells me to try again. I give it my very best shot. I still can't do it. The doctor smiles and tells me to lay back down. Then he goes into the kitchen and tells my mother that she has to get me to the hospital immediately. He says, "Mrs. Brophy, I'm afraid your son might have infantile paralysis".

It's early Spring 1949 in south Los Angeles. The war is over and there's a perceptible feeling in the air that in L.A., anything's possible. Dad works as a carpenter for the City of Los Angeles. Although money's tight, things are good. Mom is a stay-at-home mother, kept busy with three children. I'm eight years old and a handful all by myself. My sister Diane is six years old, with a birthday 2 days before mine. My brother Danny is out of diapers and walking. It's a good time to be a kid.

We live at 122 E 116th Street in Los Angeles in a small two-bedroom bungalow. Newspapers are a nickel. The ice man delivers a block of ice which keeps the ice box cold until the next delivery. I like to chase him down the street and eat the ice chips that fly when he cuts the blocks to fit the ice box. The Helms bread truck drives by the house every day. The milk man delivers ice cold milk in four glass quart bottles early in the morning several times a week. The Salk polio vaccine won't be invented for two more years. And doctors still make house calls.

After the doctor leaves, my mother calls dad and tells him he has to leave work and take me to the hospital right away. We only have one car, so dad drives us to the Los Angeles General hospital in Boyle Heights. It's the biggest building I've ever seen, 12 or 13 stories tall. As soon as we get to the hospital, they take me into a small room with a stainless-steel table in the middle.

I take off everything except my underwear and the man tells me to lay down on that table on my stomach. The table's cold. Two female nurses each grab an arm. Two male nurses each grab a leg. I'm scared to death when I see a plunger with a huge needle about 3 inches long. I scream like a banshee when they stick it into my spine. I try to escape, but they have me pinned.

Soon I hear the dreaded news. I have the virus in my spinal fluid. The polio epidemic has gotten me. I've come down with polio.

I'm taken to the polio ward on the top floor of the hospital. Everything is painted white. There's a row of beds on each side of the room and nurses seem to be everywhere, busily bustling around.

Once they have me settled in bed, a nurse comes by with a large cylindrical silver machine that she plugs into the wall and turns on. It makes a high-pitched spinning sound for several minutes. When it stops, she opens it up and takes out an olive-green army wool blanket. It's steaming hot. She wraps me in it like a cocoon. I can hardly stand it! God, how I hate that blanket. I soon find out that it will happen to me several times each day.

I later learn that it's called the 'Sister Kenny' treatment. They tell me it's the only thing they know to do to treat polio. I cry "Turn it off" whenever it's time to get wrapped and the nurse assures me that longer is better. I'll never forget that feeling.

Each day a doctor comes by, takes my temperature and checks things out. Then the dreaded machine is again brought by my bed. Rinse and repeat. This process goes on day after day and I lose track of time.

After a week and a half or two weeks, my father receives a call from the doctor who's been assigned to me. It's Wednesday morning, and he tells dad my condition is worsening, and that he might need to put me into an iron lung. The doctor needs my father's permission. My father pauses for a moment and asks him if he needs to make a decision right now, or if he can tell him tomorrow. The doctor assures him it isn't urgent and they agree to talk at 10 a.m. the following day.

Now, there's another thing you need to know. My parents are deeply religious. We all go to Grace Nazarene Church on Normandie Avenue several times every week. Sunday school and then church service every Sunday morning. Young people service and then regular Sunday evening sermon. Prayer meeting every Wednesday evening. Friday or Saturday special church events. Revival services that take place every evening for a week, several times a year. Tent meetings in between. Other than school, it's my entire organized life.

Wednesday night prayer meetings are my least favorite parts of the church schedule. A bunch, maybe 15 to 20, 'old' people all get together and meet at 7:00 p.m. They ask for prayer requests and 45 minutes or so later we get up from our knees and go home.

The Wednesday prayer meeting following dad's phone call with the doctor, he tells the group he has a special prayer request. He tells them that he believes God can heal me from polio and asks that everyone join him in that belief and pray for my healing. He later tells me that that night's meeting goes on until almost 10:30 p.m. It's never lasted that long. I, being in the polio ward at the hospital, have no idea what's going on outside of my restricted world.

The next morning the doctor comes by my bed as usual and does the same things he always does. About 15 minutes later he comes back with two other doctors. They poke, prod, test, question, and check me out for another half hour. I have no idea what's happening, except that the dreaded silver machine doesn't make its appearance that morning, or any time after that. I'm supremely grateful for that, but have no idea what's going on.

At 10:00 a.m. my father makes the promised phone call to the doctor. He tells the doctor that they prayed for my healing the night before, and if he needs to put me into an iron lung it's okay. The doctor tells him that something has happened that they can't understand. He says that they've completely checked me out that morning and I have no evidence of ever having had polio.

Dad tells the doctor that God has healed me. The doctor tells him he doesn't believe in healing, but that something has happened over the course of the night that they don't understand and medicine can't explain.

They keep me in the hospital for another two days. They run lots more tests. Nothing shows up. It's as if everything that has happened to me has been nothing more than a bad dream.

I don't know how it works. I'm not promoting any belief system, but I've learned that there is an exceptional power generated when a number of people all focus on a single subject and infuse their desire with emotion. However it works, I'm supremely grateful. It provides me with the opportunity to engage in multiple adventures with a body that never knew what might have been.

2 | The Entrepreneur Emerges

In early 1941, before World War II begins, my parents decide to leave Chicago and head West. They load everything they own, along with me in diapers, into a 1937 Chevy and point the car towards California. The mattress is tied on the roof of the car and dad has under $100 in his wallet. Dad keeps driving until he reaches the Pacific Ocean. He rents a small house about a block from the beach and we settle down in Manhattan Beach, California.

Just days after we arrive, dad goes to work at Douglas Aircraft Company in El Segundo, building the B-17 Flying Fortress bomber. In a matter of months, the Japanese attack the US Navy fleet stationed at Pearl Harbor, and dad volunteers to enlist in the Army. When the enlistment officer finds out where he's working, dad is told that he'll be a lot more valuable to the country building airplanes then he would be carrying a rifle. After the war's over, dad goes to work as a carpenter for the City of Los Angeles.

So begins my saga…

You may have already guessed that as a kid, I'm a handful. My jeans always have patched knees. Often the knees of my pants have patches on patches, both inside and outside. It's a constant struggle to keep me in tennis shoes. In a matter of weeks, I've got cardboard stuffed in the bottom of my new shoes to cover the holes I've worn through the soles in an effort to save my socks.

Mrs. Wooley, my fourth-grade teacher calls mom one evening and says, "I think Larry needs eyeglasses. He squints so tightly at the blackboard, I don't know if he can read what I'm writing". Thank God dad has good health insurance coverage with the City of Los Angeles, because it includes vision coverage. I break my glasses so often that the lady at the eye clinic knows my name.

Heck, dozens of summer days before I get out of grade school, I hop the freight trains going by our home to get a free ride to the dump. The dump is a huge undeveloped area a few miles from my home where people leave their worn-out furniture, appliances and other trash. Freight trains travel by our home through south L.A. at the leisurely pace of five miles an hour.

To a 10-year old boy, the long, slow freight trains that go by with open boxcar doors are absolutely irresistible. I run alongside the boxcars and jump into the open doors. I take along my bow and a couple of beat-up arrows and always find something to use for a target. It's actually a miracle I don't end up under one of those boxcar wheels.

I know that the last train heading back towards home passes by the dump about a half-hour before dad gets home from work. Sometimes I have to run like hell to catch that last train to make sure I don't catch hell from dad when I get back home. I don't think mom ever knows what's going on. It seems like she's always busy with my younger brother and two younger sisters. By the way, that 'dump' I used to roam is now covered with a golf course and back-to-back expensive homes.

However, the story of every budding entrepreneur has a beginning.

I begin my entrepreneurial career early. It happens because I want things that take money. My family, like many others, struggles financially. For many years, Dad works two 40-hour a week jobs to keep the family fed and me in shoes. We kids do our chores, but there's rarely any allowance money to pass around. We're simply expected to pitch in. So, I learn early that the only way to get some change in my pocket is to find something I can do that I'll get paid for.

By the time I'm 10 years old, I find that I can sell newspapers. Not on a bicycle newspaper route like my friends, but hawking the Daily Mirror News on the corner of Main Street and Imperial Highway during evening rush hour. I run out between the lanes of traffic whenever the traffic light turns red and wave the newspapers at the drivers, shouting out the daily headline. On a good day I can make a dollar. That's really big money and I have no problem spending it.

In grade school, I'm a good student and am skipped ahead one semester in the fifth grade. It doesn't seem to make much difference to me at the time, but becomes a liability when I start high school a year younger and more immature than most of my classmates.

By the time my sister Martie comes along, our little bungalow is bursting at the seams. Dad seems to always complain about how the blacks are moving closer to our home. I remember the evening he rants, "They're only two blocks away and we have to get out of here". Dad isn't a racist. His is just the mentality of the time.

Shortly thereafter dad finds a tiny house at 3614 8th Avenue. It's really small, but he feels he can add on a couple of rooms to make it work for our family. The house is termite riddled and dad spends many hours under the house with a modified grease gun pumping arsenic into holes he drills into the floor joists. With my help, he adds a living room on the front of the house and another bedroom and laundry room in the rear.

When I'm 11 years old, a door-to-door Watkins salesman comes by the house with spices, ointments, liniments and a variety of personal items. He likes me and asks, "Hey Larry, would you like to go to work for me?". I'm always ready for an adventure, especially if it means a little extra money.

I become his delivery service. Each week he brings a box of items to the house along with a list of addresses for each item. It's my job to make sure that each item gets to the right person. I've never met so many old women in my life! And, I'll never forget the smell of lilac, which seems to permeate everything. That job lasts almost a year.

During that time, I'm a voracious reader. Our home is only four blocks from the local library. I think I've read every science fiction book on the shelves. I usually check out 8 or 10 books every other week, and always read 3 or 4 of them simultaneously.

One day in the library I pick up a magazine and see an ad about how you can make extra money selling Christmas greeting cards to your neighbors. I respond, and two weeks later the company sends me a big box of sample Christmas cards. That becomes my next entrepreneurial adventure.

For two years, after the fall semester starts, I walk door to door proudly displaying my sample cards. I guess I probably visit every house within a half mile of our home. In L.A., that's a lot of houses. I certainly hear the word, "NO" a lot. I don't make much money, but it's good experience. However, I take time to have fun, too.

Our home is 11 miles from the beach at Playa del Rey. Dad loves to surf fish and has a big, long surf casting rod. He makes a sand crab seine and we go under the Santa Monica beach pier and catch the soft-shelled sand crabs he uses for bait.

I get my own big, long fishing pole and we spend many evenings casting into the surf. Every now and then we bring home fresh bass or corvina for dinner. I love the ocean and go as often as I can. However, again, money is the impetus for my next endeavor.

By age 13 I'm riding my rickety bike to the beach to go fishing 3 or 4 days each week, all summer long. Mom usually makes a couple of sandwiches for me to bring along.

Frankly, I think she's glad to get me out of the house. I tie a big wooden tackle box on the back of my bike along with mom's lunch bag. I ride 11 miles to the beach and 11 miles back home, holding onto my fishing pole with one hand.

What a way to spend the summer! I bet I make that trip a hundred times over the course of a couple of summers. I love to fish for smelt, and my favorite bait is shrimp that costs $0.26 per box at the bait store, including tax.

But it takes money to buy bait. So, I start a lawn mowing business. I walk up and down the blocks around my neighborhood with my push mower, looking for lawns with overgrown grass. I offer to cut their lawn for a dollar. That's enough to buy bait for a couple of days with enough left over to buy a couple of Cokes and a five-cent Three Musketeers bar. I enjoy these adventures until I start high school.

Susan Miller Dorsey High School is two miles from my home, and I walk to school every day. The internal game I play walking to and from high school is to close my eyes and count the number of steps I can walk before I have to open my eyes, fall off the curb or run into a telephone pole. It's no wonder I sprain my ankles so many times.

High school isn't the high point of my life. I'm taking college prep courses that includes 3 years each of math and science and 2 years of Latin. After two semesters of chemistry, Dr. Jaffre, my chemistry teacher, asks me to be his assistant the following semester. Although I'm a slightly better than average student, my senior year I'm not very conscientious. I eventually graduate with a 2.92 GPA.

I attempt to play football, but I'm undersized and end up with a bruised kidney from a knee in the back. I pee blood for a couple of days. When that happens, mom puts her foot down and that ends my athletic career.

However, I love to sing and spend the final two and a half years in the high school acapella choir. I try out for and am selected for the all-Southern California high school choir. I join 600 students from all over Southern California and sing for the music educators national convention at the Shrine Auditorium. A couple of months later I sing with the choir for the Easter sunrise service at the Hollywood Bowl.

With four children at home money is always tight. If I want anything, I have to work for it. With the high school job coach's help, I find a job at a metal shop afternoons, Saturdays and summers for the final two years of high school. Russ, the owner, teaches me to weld, use a metal brake, and spin and polish metal on a lathe. I enjoy the work and get pretty good at it. Eventually Russ pays me on a piece-work basis so I can make a few extra dollars each week.

As dad is self-taught, he expects me to follow in his footsteps. When I talk with him about continuing on to college, he says, "Why do you want to do that? Don't expect me to pay for you to go to college. Just get a job like everybody else."

Even though I'm a math/science major and have taken every college prep course in high school, I don't continue my formal education. I get a job instead.

As an independent 17-year old, I can't stand the restrictions of family life. So, I stage an argument with mom and move out of the house. I rent a room in a big Victorian home near downtown L.A. and learn to live on my own.

I spend the days working at a couple of no-brainer jobs and in the evenings, I go roller skating at the Hollywood Roller Bowl. For several months, I skate six evenings a week because the rink in closed on Mondays. That's where I meet Donna Otto, a tall girl from Oklahoma who ends up being my first wife and the mother of our four children. But, that's a story for little later.

This is a time between wars. The Korean War is over. Vietnam isn't yet on the horizon. Although I don't know what I want to do with my life, I know that I don't want to spend two or three years in the military.

So, I decide to enlist in the California Army National Guard. I join a quartermaster supply company in the 40th Armored Division, headquartered in Torrance California. That way, I'll only have to spend 6 months on active duty and can then serve another five and a half years in the active reserve.

At the age of 18, I join the Army and become a soldier.

3 | Army National Guard Years

Army life can be either good or bad. It's all a matter of your own personal choice. If you go along with the discipline and orders you receive, no matter how you'd do it if you were in charge, it's easy. If you kick against the system, it's both painful and disagreeable.

In August 1959 I'm assigned to Fort Ord, California near Monterey to begin basic training and my 6 months of active duty service. Fortunately, I choose to go along with the system and find Army life easy and not particularly difficult.

I learn if you keep your boots shined, learn how to make a bed with the blanket so tight you can bounce a quarter off of it, and say "Yes Sir!" whenever you're told to do something, it's a breeze. I qualify 'Expert' with the M1 rifle, peel several hundred-pound sacks of potatoes during KP duty, and learn how to handle a 'deuce-and-a-half', the 2.5-ton Army truck.

After the initial eight weeks of basic training, we get the weekend off. I decide to hitch-hike the 300 miles from Fort Ord to Hollywood where I'm able to spend a few hours with my girlfriend Donna. Then I hitch-hike back to Fort Ord, making sure to arrive before the Sunday 8:00 p.m. curfew. I repeat that hitch-hiking odyssey another half-dozen times before my 6 months of active duty is completed. In February of 1960, I leave Fort Ord for the last time.

Finally, ready to start my adult life, I need a job. After a couple of temporary shipping-clerk stints with hardware and drafting supply companies, I apply to Pacific Bell. They offer me a job as a messenger, driving envelopes full of company documents between the many PacBell facilities. That position lasts 6 months until they suggest they think I'm better suited to go into the Commercial Division.

Soon I join the coin division and start emptying coins from pay phones throughout Southern California. After a few months of driving through some of the seediest parts of Los Angeles, they move me into the coin counting operation. Down in the basement of the building, I'm one of about 15 young guys running the machines that count tens of thousands of dollars of nickels, dimes and quarters daily.

However, while this is going on in my work life, my personal life takes a major detour. My girlfriend is pregnant. The mores of the day dictate that marriage is the only honorable thing to do. On Saturday, December 3, 1960 Donna Otto and I become husband and wife.

As my car is a on its last legs, dad tells me he is giving us his 1957 Plymouth Savoy as a wedding gift. It's a stick shift and its only problem is that the overdrive doesn't work properly. I don't care. I'm both grateful and amazed at his generosity.

We don't have much money, so we decide to celebrate our marriage with a Saturday one-night honeymoon at Big Bear Lake. When we awake on Sunday morning, I'm shocked to discover 4 or 5 inches of snow on the ground. I get into the car to warm it up and press the brake pedal. It goes all the way down to the floor and the smell of brake fluid is strong.

Oh-oh. That's a problem.

Sunday and five inches of snow means there aren't any repair shops open and I absolutely have to be at work Monday morning. I'm able to drive that car all the way down the curvy mountain road with no brakes, using only low gear and the emergency brake to slow down. As you can imagine, there are more than a few tense moments.

Late Sunday evening when I get down the hill, dad meets me on I-10 with a rebuilt master brake cylinder. I'm able to replace it and bleed the brakes. Although this isn't a particularly auspicious start to married life, it's definitely a memorable experience.

We rent an apartment in Hollywood. A few months later, Steve makes his appearance at Hollywood Presbyterian hospital on March 29, 1961. I'm a father at the age of 20. I still remember the light blue Naugahyde covered chairs in the expectant fathers' waiting area and the 6-month old hunting and fishing magazines that litter the room. It's amazing how quickly your priorities change!

We move into a small two-bedroom home in Baldwin Park, CA and I'm getting bored with my job. I'm one of the top coin counters down in the basement at PacBell, but the regimen of doing the same thing day after day is making me very antsy.

I begin looking at the want ads for something that might bring some excitement and more money into my life. I find one that looks very interesting.

Certified Life Insurance Co, selling White Cross health insurance, is looking for agents. The ad says you can make $500 a week and offers to help qualified applicants get an insurance sales license. I apply for the job and after a couple of months, become a licensed 'Life and Disability' insurance agent.

I resign from PacBell and start selling health insurance. What a change! Each day I put on my only suit and am given 'leads' to follow up on.

After 4 months, I'm the third from the top selling agent of the 20 agents in my office. Because I'm doing so well, the manager starts giving me more leads to follow up on; insurance lapse notices and claim payment check copies. That proves to be both his and my undoing. After learning that the customers aren't receiving what they think they're insured for, my production goes through the floor.

I can't sell something I don't believe in. Two monthsn later, I resign and have to find another job.

I learn that the debit division of the Prudential Insurance Co is hiring in Whittier, CA and move my insurance license there. They pay a small base salary plus commissions.

It's a brutal experience, collecting nickels and dimes weekly and selling mortgage insurance whenever possible. My debit is 20 miles from my home in a new section of Whittier. I really hate this job.

We live in one of four tiny 2-bedroom rental units behind a residential home in Baldwin Park. One weekend my young next-door neighbor and I have a couple of beers together. He tells me he's making way more money than me as a roof stacker. A roof stacker is the carpenter that puts up the rafters on a new home. My neighbor says he's working on a piece work basis, getting paid for each roof he stacks. He says he'll teach me the ropes.

I don't take him up on it until my manager, Bert Tippie, lies to me. Twice. He tells me he'll meet me at a specific coffee shop in Whittier at 9:00 a.m. and never shows up. The second time it happens a couple of days later, I quit and tell my new friend I'm ready to go to work.

I'm now self-employed and travel around Southern California looking for new tracts of homes under construction. Population and homes are exploding all over. I look for the project superintendent, see if they need a roof stacker and ask how much they're paying per house. I can stack the roof of one house a day and make $50 to $75 per home. That's really good money in the early 1960's.

I get to the job site before dawn with a full thermos of coffee and wait until it's light enough to toss the rafters up on the joists and get to work. I frame one roof every day. The part of roof stacking I find most enjoyable is that when I go up to a house, it's simply a box. When I leave, it has a roof and looks like a home.

During this time, our birth control effort is the rhythm method. It didn't work. On February 10, 1963 Julie comes along. We are now a family of four. Now that we know that the rhythm method isn't foolproof, Donna starts using the vaginal foam birth control method. We soon learn that that method doesn't work either. On December 18, 1964 Jennifer is born.

During this time, my National Guard service is two Thursday nights a month plus an annual two-week summer camp which takes place out in the desert at a place called Hunter Liggett. I've been promoted to each higher rank as soon as Army regulations will allow. By now I'm the platoon sergeant of our supply company's 40-man Headquarters platoon. I get to chase after all the loafers and am pegged to run the training classes.

The officers in my unit encourage me to go to OCS and become a lieutenant, but I have to agree to three additional years of US Army service. There's absolutely no way that's in my cards.

Every night after our bi-weekly Guard meetings, I head down to the bowling alley along with the other sergeants and a few officers to knock down a couple of cold ones. I learn that our company commander, Capt. Larry Cantrell, is also a carpenter. We like each other and start doing piece work as a team. We work well together. Larry was raised in Arkansas and has a lot of family members still living there. One night just before my 6-year reserve obligation is over, he gets really serious.

He says, "Larry, you and I know how homes are built here in Southern California. In Arkansas, they're at least 50 years behind us. If we go to Arkansas, knowing what we know about building, we can get rich building homes."

Wow! This sounds like an incredible opportunity! We decide to both move to Arkansas and make our fortune. Dad builds a trailer, we load up all of our worldly possessions and head out to Stuttgart, Arkansas.

Larry Cantrell, Donna, the kids and I all pile into my Chevy pickup, with Larry and I changing drivers so we won't have to stop for anything other than gas. While Larry is driving through Utah, he suddenly shouts. I glance into the side mirror in time to see the trailer driving all alone on the road behind us. The hitch has broken off of the box.

In seconds, it veers to the right and noses into a ditch on the side of the road. Everything is catapulted into the air. The portable dishwasher ends up stuck in the middle of a clump of trees about 10 feet off the ground. The rest of our stuff is spread over a couple of acres. It looks like a bomb has exploded. What a freaking disaster!

While Larry goes to the nearest town and rents a smaller trailer, Donna and I spend a couple of hours picking through our belongings. The trailer, a busted-up dresser and broken and smashed furniture odds and ends are left by the side of the road. The dishwasher remains wedged in the trees.

We find the six case-hardened bolts that dad used to attach the trailer box to the hitch in the middle of the road. Each is snapped cleanly in half.

Shaken but undeterred, we get back on the road. When we arrive in Arkansas, Larry and I start a general contracting company and name it Ambassador Builders. All we have to do now is find a place to live and something to build.

4 | Arkansas

We begin driving to Arkansas on August 5, 1965, a couple of days after I'm discharged from the California Army National Guard. I'm 24 years old. Larry Cantrell was discharged from Active Reserve with the rank of Captain a couple of days earlier. We're both going to be on Inactive Reserve status for the following two years.

On August 11, 1965, on the corner of 116th Street about four blocks east of the home where I grew up, police arrest a drunk young black man. The arrest turns sour. In fact, it gets so bad that over 30 people lose their life before it's over. It's the Watts riots, and the California National Guard is called in to keep the peace.

We watch the news on TV intently. We see images of the guys in our unit driving through the streets carrying loaded machine guns and rifles. Both Larry and I are certain that the Guard is going to call us back as our unit as is one of the first to get involved in the peace keeping effort. The riot lasts five or six days and we breathe a huge sigh of relief when it ends without receiving a phone call.

My partner, Larry, selected Stuttgart because he has family here and is sure we can get a business going quickly. Larry's left his family in California and wants to send for his wife and four children as quickly as he can. In a couple of months, the Cantrell family finally all gets back together.

Donna and I rent a home in Stuttgart at 610 S Leslie St. I find some used furniture and quickly settle in. The home seems perfect for us. It has three bedrooms and a living room with a big old brick fireplace in the living room. However, late summer is peak mosquito season in rice country, and I find that I'm allergic to mosquito bites. A bite makes a huge welt that itches for a week or more.

I spend two or three nights flailing around half the night with the bedroom light on, trying to kill the mosquitos that keep buzzing around my head. I finally find that they're coming down the fireplace chimney through a damper that won't close completely. I'm able to cover the top of the chimney with a piece of window screen, solving my night-time mosquito problem.

Arkansas is a lot different than California, and Stuttgart, a town of 10,000 people, is like being on another planet compared to L.A. It's muggy in the summer and snows in the winter. There's never any traffic and the primary industry is rice farming. Stuttgart is nicknamed the rice and duck capital of the world. After a short time, I call it the rice, duck and mosquito capital of the world. Surrounded by farms and rice fields, the mosquito population must be in the billions.

Main Street is only 2 or 3 blocks long, with small businesses lining each side of the street. It seems like everybody knows everybody else. It takes five or ten minutes to walk a block because everyone waves at you and wants to talk about the weather or how you're doing.

In Los Angeles, you're lucky if you know your next-door neighbor.

I've never met so many friendly people before in my life. Stuttgart is a prosperous town with newer cars and trucks and neat, well-cared for homes with manicured lawns a block or two off the main drag. I discover there are dozens of churches in town along with one bank and one Savings and Loan.

As Larry's a Southern Baptist, he immediately joins the largest church in town and starts networking. I join a tiny, brand-new Church of the Nazarene with a couple dozen members and a pastor about my age just out of seminary. However, as I have a family, the most pressing issue for me is finding a way to bring in some money.

In a matter of days, we find a fantastic way to blend our work ethic and skillset. Jim Walter Homes, headquartered in Little Rock, is the largest shell home builder in the South. Their model is to build a shell home on your property with no plumbing, electricity, insulation or sheetrock and no exterior finish. The finished product is simply a block pier foundation holding up a framed structure built according to the blueprint.

The finished shell home includes the foundation, walls and exterior sheathing, doors and windows, and a composition shingle roof. The finish of the remainder of the home is left to the property owner themself. Jim Walter customers are those folks who can't afford a home, but want their own place to live.

Most of the Jim Walter homes are way out in the sticks. There are typically no local contractors available, so they hire workers who are willing to travel to and stay in the boondocks. While the work is supposed to comply with the Uniform Building Code standards, no building inspections are involved. The best part for us is that they have a backlog of work and a shortage of qualified people. That's where we come in.

Over the course of the next two or three months, Larry Cantrell and I build six shell homes together. We get an address – or more often, a location like "turn left at the yellow flag and follow the dirt driveway to the end" – and a starting date.

We load our sleeping bags, a camping stove, cans of food and a change of underwear into my pickup truck and take off. Almost all of the homes we build are in the Ozarks, in the heavily wooded, rolling hills covering the northwest part of the state. The homes are small, typically around a thousand square feet.

The best part was that we get paid as soon as each shell home is complete.

When we get to a building site, we locate the stake the owner has driven into the ground showing where he wants his home, and wait for the building supplies to arrive. It's always the same. We hear the sound of a lumbering truck, straining and overweight, loaded with everything we need. The driver winches up the front of the truck bed, unceremoniously drops everything on the ground, unstraps the load and leaves.

By the time the load hits the dirt, we've already looked at the plans and have the foundation lined out. We start work at dawn and work until it gets too dark to see. Larry and I can put a completed shell home on a bare piece of ground in six or seven days. The Jim

Walter people are amazed and really disappointed when we tell them we have to quit and do other work.

The first custom home we build in Stuttgart is for the preacher of my church. He bought a lot in a tiny new subdivision for a couple thousand dollars. I draw up a house plan and have a blueprint made. We build a complete small three-bedroom home with a brick exterior for him for a turnkey price of $8,000.

We hire an old (to us) black man in his 50's as a laborer to give us a hand. Although we barely make any profit on that first home, we each generate a living wage for a couple of months.

Ironically, the largest and oldest Stuttgart building contractor has just started work on a home directly behind the preacher's house. They're framing the floor joists about two weeks before we even break ground. We watch in amazement as it takes 3 or 4 men working with ladders a day to frame a couple of walls.

We end up putting the roof on the preacher's home over a month before they do.

However, we learn a very important lesson on that first home. We're stymied by the other trades we need. We learn that the plumbers in Stuttgart have one pace. Slow.

The same is true for the electrician, the bricklayer and painter. In fact, all of the other building trades. While we're able to complete the carpentry in blazing, Southern California style, we have to deal with the slow southern pace of everyone else. It looks like the path to riches is going to be a marathon instead of a sprint.

At the small church I attend I meet Jack, a guy about my age, with a glass eye. He lost his eye when he was 10 years old. He was throwing darts at a tree when a dart bounced back and hit him in his left eye. Jack works for one of the big local farmers in the rice fields repairing levees. He keeps telling me what great fishing there is around Stuttgart so we decide to go fishing for catfish one night with a lantern. I tell him I'll pick him up at the rice field he's working.

When I get there about dusk, I see him busily working to repair a levee breech with a shovel. He's wearing a white T-shirt, but the back of his shirt looks black. It's totally covered with mosquitos. He finishes working, shakes off his T-shirt and we head out to fish. I don't recall if we caught anything that evening, but can't ever forget seeing all those mosquitos on his back.

We build the next custom home for a young family that goes to Larry's church across the street from the preacher's lot. I draw the plans for that home as well. We use the lessons we've learned about all the local sub-contractors and end up making a decent profit. The young couple's very pleased and proudly show their dream home to all of their friends.

This gives us some great positive recognition and we're able to bid on a large 3,000 square foot home for the Superintendent of the Stuttgart School District. The only other bidder is the long-established builder that built the home that we worked circles around behind the preacher's house. We bid $85,000 and are ecstatic when we win the contract.

This is a big deal. We know this could be the springboard we need to really make a name for Ambassador Builders. It's an incredible home with solid cherry kitchen cabinets and solid cherry paneling in a huge game room with 10-foot ceiling, wet bar and guest bath.

We hire an old retired cabinet maker to build the kitchen cabinets and install the paneling. His work is flawless and we make a nice profit. The Superintendent is most impressed with the quality of his new home. We're happy and sure we're on the path to success.

While his home is being completed, we're able to bid on and win contracts to build two additional homes. However, the local banking system is in turmoil in 1966. The United States is still in the midst of the Cold War. As usual, the contracts are contingent upon the owners obtaining a home loan.

In California, the usual lending process is for a Savings and Loan to make the construction loan, and upon completion, the bank makes the permanent home loan. Home lending in Stuttgart is exactly opposite. The bank makes the construction loan and the S&L makes the permanent loan.

Our problem is that the only bank in Stuttgart has run out of money. Financing isn't available for any new construction loans. That means that in the fall of 1966, our business comes to a screeching halt.

We're able to do some minor remodeling and repair work for a few months, but the writing is on the wall. I sell my interest in the tools and equipment we've accumulated to Larry Cantrell for pennies on the dollar and rent a trailer in Little Rock.

Donna, the kids and I load up all of our worldly belongings and again hit the road. This time, its back to California.

5 | The Insurance Agent

Even though we don't have a place to live and no income on the immediate horizon, it's a big relief getting back to California. The trip back from Arkansas has been uneventful. We have enough money for a deposit and the first month's rent on a small house we find in Escondido.

As soon as the trailer is unloaded and returned to the rental yard, I buy all of the newspapers in San Diego county and start scouring the want ads.

I deliver phone books for a few days. Another few days are spent on the dumb end of a shovel. I'll do anything it takes to make a buck. After a couple of weeks, I see an ad in the San Diego Union that looks promising. The John E. Wood General Agency of the John Hancock Insurance Co. is looking for insurance agents for a small satellite office in Oceanside, CA.

I drive to San Diego and, after a verbal interview, am given a comprehensive Myers-Briggs battery of tests to determine whether I'm likely to be a successful insurance agent. A week later, they call and tell me they want to hire me. I learn I've scored the second highest number on that battery of tests that they've ever received.

I'm sent to the John Hancock Insurance Co Home Office in Boston the following week to join about 40 other new agents from around the country for a weeklong 'New Agent' training class. It's my first time on a commercial airplane, a Boeing 707.

The plane lands, slipping and sliding, at Logan International Airport in bitter cold the last week of January. I take a cab to the assigned hotel, a couple of blocks from the imposing Home Office building, looking forward to my new adventure.

One evening, half way through the training class, I get bored in the hotel room and decide to see if there's anything going on. I step out of the hotel right into the teeth of a nor'easter blizzard. It's my first experience with one. The wind is blowing the snow sideways and you can barely see the other side of the street. I'm sure not going to go very far.

Half way down the block I find some stairs heading down to a comedy club and decide to go down for a drink. George Carlin is performing tonight. I don't know who he is, but the club is packed. I'm really naive, and this guy really has a nasty mouth. After a couple of drinks, I pipe up and say, "Where'd you get your couth?"

George Carlin immediately says, "I'm glad you asked me that question. I'm a proud graduate of the Sam Houston Institute of Technology." He then breaks into the college cheer. "Sam Houston. Sam Houston. Sam Houston Institute of Technology. S. H. I. T., S. H. I. T.", and on and on. Everyone, including me, laughs our butt off.

One thing I can say for sure about John Hancock. They're meticulous and thorough in their training. I enjoy the week and it goes by fast. When the week training is completed, they announce a contest to see which of the 40 agents can write the highest number of new insurance policies over the following 10 weeks.

I return to Oceanside, California adjacent to Camp Pendleton, a large U.S. Marine Corps training base. The Vietnam War is going full force and both U.S. Marines and Navy hospital corpsmen are being readied for a tour of duty in Vietnam. When I get back from Boston, I'm introduced to the other agents in our small Oceanside office. The office consists of a sales manager and three other agents, mostly retired military.

I'm the new kid on the block. Literally.

While my business career is budding, Donna and I have another budding taking place. Donna misses a couple of periods and, sure enough, we're expecting yet another child. As oral contraceptives are still brand new and their safety is being challenged, we use the diaphragm birth control method. We learn that that method isn't foolproof either. On July 12, 1967, Lori, our fourth and final child, is born. We decide to surgically prevent another unexpected surprise.

Meanwhile, my insurance career gets a start from an unexpected source. Our office receives a few mail-in insurance inquiries from young men that are training at the U.S. Naval Hospital at Camp Pendleton, getting ready for their tour in Vietnam. I volunteer to follow-up on them.

I check onto the Camp Pendleton Marine Corps base and go into the Navy hospital corpsmen's barracks in the evenings. It's really a no-brainer to write dozens of $10,000 life insurance policies over the following weeks. I easily win the 10-week "new agent" contest. I never learn how many of the families of those Navy corpsmen that I write policies for end up collecting their sons' life insurance.

Now a successful 28-year old insurance agent with a growing family, we're able to buy a small 3-bedroom home at 4102 Lewis St in Oceanside. Although it's a small tract home, it's a huge improvement over the rental home we've been shoe-horned into.

By late June 1968 my younger brother, Daniel R. Brophy, an Army Spec4, is serving in Vietnam as a helicopter repairman. He's an exceptionally gifted mechanic and has been in Vietnam for several months. Sitting alone in the small Oceanside office early one afternoon the last week of June, I receive a dreadful phone call. I'm told Danny has been killed in Vietnam.

I'm overcome with grief and can't stop the tears flowing down my cheeks.

A short time later that afternoon the phone rings again. The main Agency office in San Diego has an urgent matter that has to be attended to immediately. A young U.S. Navy corpsman just called their office and says he's shipping out to Vietnam the following day. He says it's imperative that he get the beneficiary designation changed on his John Hancock insurance policy. It falls upon me to dry my tears and drive out to Camp Pendleton to meet him in his barracks and complete the change of beneficiary request.

Going onto the base that day is the hardest thing I've ever done in my life. I can't stop grieving for Danny, and seeing all the young Marines is almost more than I can bear. I take care of the requested beneficiary change and drive back to the office to turn it in.

Sadly, I learn two weeks later that the young man that I went out to see was also killed in Vietnam.

My mother subsequently receives a post-humous U.S. Army Silver Star medal, the Army's second highest award for bravery. Danny died a hero, but nothing can bring him back. You don't need to ask why I oppose war. Nor do you need ask why I never went back onto the base at Camp Pendleton.

I've always wanted to continue my education, but due to the increasing responsibilities of fatherhood, never seem to have the opportunity. This seems like a good time to re-ignite that desire, so I enroll at Palomar Junior College and begin taking 2 or 3 daytime college courses per semester.

Most of my insurance appointments are in the evening, so Tuesday and Thursday mornings are devoted to classes and study. I end up with 20+ credit hours before focusing entirely again on my career.

Not content with work and college, I find and purchase a pan-handle, ravine lot in Oceanside. I draw up plans for a tri-level 3-bedroom home large enough for all of us. I apply for and received a building loan.

Working spare hours and weekends, by August, 1969 I complete our new home at 204 N Hoover St.

During this time, I find myself spending a lot of time helping public school teachers set up tax-sheltered annuities. I'm also introduced to a law firm that specialized in trusts and estate planning services. My first year with the John E. Wood Agency ends with the award of "New Agent of the Year".

My second year ends with being recognized "Co-Agent of the Year". During this period, I also obtain a Series 7 NASD Registered Representative securities license and began selling mutual funds. My career is taking off.

The preeminent professional designation in the life insurance industry is that of Certified Life Underwriter. It gives the recipient the right to add the title, 'CLU' to their name. It's awarded by The American College in Bryn Mawr, Pennsylvania upon completion of a five-year study course on ethics, law, pensions and estate planning. Each year of the course entails reading and digesting a stack of books inches thick, followed by a 3-hour exam at the end of each year.

I decide to become a CLU.

However, having always been impatient, at this point in my life I can't see five years down the road. So, I decide that I'm going to complete the five-year Certified Life Underwriter course in two years. As I don't have enough patience to read the thousands of pages, I skim the books and bluff my way through the hours-long exams. I pass every course and receive the coveted CLU designation. My grade scores certainly didn't put me at the top of the class, but I'm now a CLU.

Working with attorneys specializing in retirement and estate planning introduces me to a securities and financial services firm specializing in financial planning. It's the Ralph S. Wilford Company, a small licensed broker-dealer headquartered in La Mesa, California.

They have an incredibly effective marketing approach. The firm sponsors bi-weekly financial planning dinner seminars at the Hanalei Hotel in San

Diego's Mission Valley. The seminars are held in the largest room in the hotel and each seminar usually has between 100 and 200 attendees. A complimentary meal is followed by an hour presentation on the uses of money. I attend a dinner seminar and am blown away by its effectiveness.

I meet with Mr. Wilford and the other principals of the firm and, at the age of 29, decide to join their firm as a financial planner.

6 | Financial Services Unlimited

When I inform John Wood, the General Agent, that I'll be leaving John Hancock he's disappointed, but very supportive. My fellow insurance agents all wish me good luck in my new adventure. Fran Leland and Marge West, two top insurance agent partners are my friends and give me a small wooden plaque inscribed with "Illegitimi non carborundum". They say it's their advice for me: "Don't let the bastards wear you down". That plaque hangs on my wall for years.

The Ralph S. Wilford Company office is over 40 miles from my home in Oceanside. The bi-weekly financial planning seminars at the Hanalei hotel are the same distance. I make that trip daily for the better part of a year. I enjoy the environment and the opportunity to genuinely help people with their family finances. I learn a tremendous amount and do well financially.

The only problem is that the seminars are all held 40 miles away, and many of my prospective clients find it difficult to travel that distance.

I offer to open a branch office of the Ralph S. Wilford Company in Oceanside. They approve and say that before it can happen, I need to obtain a NASD Series 24 Registered Principal license. In California, the tests are given on Mondays in San Francisco a couple of times a year, so I register to take the next test.

The Wilford Co. registers me in a training class the weekend preceding the test. The class consisted of two days taking many sample tests, learning the correct answer to every one of 150 questions likely to be on the official NASD test. I memorize the correct answer to every multiple-choice question.

On Monday I go into a room and join 50 other people taking the three and a half-hour exam. I complete the exam in just under than two hours, including a review of each of my answers. I exit the testing room 40 minutes ahead of the next person. Although test scores aren't provided, I know that I haven't missed a single question.

The Wilford Company financial planning seminars are presented with an overhead projector using acetate slides. Willing to attempt to present the seminar in North San Diego County myself, I make a copy of the acetates and buy an overhead projector. I rent an event room at the Lake San Marcos Country Club and begin conducting dinner seminars. They're initially small, typically 15-25 people per seminar.

I invite Phil Jauregui, a young insurance buddy who sells insurance with Northwestern Mutual to attend one of my seminars. He gets hooked and we decide to start our own financial planning firm. He studies for and passes the Series 7 NASD Registered Representative exam.

Our new corporation is named Financial Services Unlimited, Inc., and I'm installed as president.

We rent a small office and refer to the company as 'FSU'. Our new company grows rapidly. At the time, we're the only full-service financial planning company operating in North San Diego County.

We soon begin putting together real estate limited partnerships. I add a significant section to the bi-weekly seminars regarding the benefits of including real estate as part of your overall financial strategy. The real estate investments are structured so that FSU is entitled to receive a small annual management fee and 25% of all profits after the investors have received their entire investment back plus ten percent.

Property values are sky-rocketing in North San Diego County. Some of the local communities are increasing in value as much as 20% a year. You don't have to be especially brilliant to do well in that market environment and our clients do very well indeed.

We add additional Registered Representatives as financial planners and FSU prospers. We quickly out-grow our small office space. Two young Registered Reps, Joe Vosmik and Carl Anderson, each join the firm and became minority shareholders.

Joe is good friends with Carl and had invited him to one of our investment seminars. Joe is a high-energy guy with an engaging smile and easy-going manner.

Carl has a real driver-type personality and always wears his Phi Beta Kappa pin. He's proud that he graduated near the top of his class at SMU and always let everyone know. He has a lot of ego and always describes himself as "A Phi Beta Kappa from SMU".

After he joins the firm, he assumes the role of sales manager. It obviously rankles him that I'm the president of the company while he's the one with the most prestigious educational chops.

I draw upon my earlier experience as a contractor and we begin construction of a new 10,000 square foot office building on El Camino Real in Oceanside. The project is structured as an investment for our clients and is completed within the projected timeline and under budget. A couple thousand square feet are leased by FSU and become the center of our operations.

While all of this is transpiring, my personal life is experiencing significant stress. I was – and still am – a work-a-holic. I can't begin to imagine the frustration that Donna must have felt, with a husband who appears more married to his business than his family. I'm oblivious to the gap that's developing between us.

I describe our marriage as being like two cars driving side-by-side down the road, each travelling 50 miles an hour. For years, we travel the road together. Then, slowly and imperceptibly, my car starts going a little faster. My life experiences become richer and deeper, while she remains at home as the mother to our four children.

She was, and still is, a wonderful woman and mother. However, as my car gains speed and begins travelling at 51 miles an hour, after a few years the gulf between us grows so wide that I can't even see her in the rearview mirror. In 1972, our marriage of 12 years comes to an end and we decide to go our separate ways.

I move out of the home I've built and spend a couple of weeks sharing a very small apartment in Del Mar with an old friend, Dick Parsons. Dick is my age, never married, with a funny, quirky sense of humor.

Soon after, I find and rent an apartment in Cardiff, California and settle in.

When our divorce is finalized, I deed the home to Donna and support her and our children until they all eventually become 18 years old. I continue to remain close to my children and spend every other weekend with them for many years.

The purpose of financial planning is to make sure you can retire comfortably, while providing protection for your family should you not live to retirement. The financial tools of banks, insurance, securities and real estate are used to accomplish these goals. Attorneys are used to provide the legal instruments of wills and trusts.

One of the physicians that provides the insurance exams that are often required of our clients is Dr. Alan Duff. He's tall and raw-boned, about 10 years older than me. His doctor's office is just down the street in Carlsbad. Alan has a gruff demeanor and a big bushy mustache, but is genuinely caring and easy to speak with.

I call him to schedule a physical for a client shortly after becoming newly single. He tells me that his office manager is also newly single and suggests I call and invite her to lunch. I call her and we hit it off immediately. Her name is Jeannie Galland and she has 3 children about the same age as mine.

After dating for two or three months, we decide to rent a home together in Del Mar. I'm now dad to four biological children and an unofficial dad to three more.

By now, FSU is profitably humming along and we're receiving calls regarding investment opportunities for our clients on a regular basis. One of the people we meet with is a representative of a venture capital firm headquartered in Los Angeles. We've been recommended to them as an affiliate, providing their services to new businesses in San Diego County looking for startup capital.

After discussing the offer, my partners and I decide it's worth exploring. They suggest I'm probably the one best qualified to take the lead. A month later, we rent an executive office on the 14th floor of the US National Bank building in San Diego.

I continue presenting the financial planning seminars. By now they've grown in size to over 100 people per seminar on a bi-weekly basis. While dividing my time between our Oceanside office and the exccutive suite in San Diego, I place ads in the San Diego Union newspaper offering venture capital and field the calls that come in.

If the opportunity seems like it might be worth following up, I schedule an interview in San Diego. For the first couple of months, I make occasional trips for appointments and submit a couple of applications to the venture capital firm without results.

One day I receive a call from a gent with a strong Australian accent. His name is Pete Francis. He says he's invented a machine that will revolutionize the mining industry. He calls it an autogenous impact air mill.

I don't know a thing about mining and it means nothing to me. I'm skeptical and don't think it's worth my time, but he's insistent. Pete says he has a working model and wants to show me how it works. I agree to meet him the following day in the parking lot of the hotel at which he's staying.

The next day I meet him for the first time. He's a short man, with a ruddy complexion and twinkling blue eyes. The machine isn't impressive until he starts it up and drops a box of glass bottles, one at a time, into the opening on the top. In seconds the bottles are turned into fine sand.

I can't believe what I just saw. Pete said that the niche he wants to exploit is hard rock gold mining, where the biggest problem is crushing the ore fine enough to extract the fine gold the ore contains.

He tells me he only needs a couple hundred thousand dollars to begin manufacturing his mills. I tell him I want to show it to Roger Quast, a stock broker friend I know who has some experience with manufacturing start-ups.

Roger's been working for a mid-sized securities firm in San Diego for the past 6 years. I was introduced to him by one of my old fellow insurance agent friends who thinks very highly of him. Roger's about 6'-2" tall with curly brown hair and an easy, out-going manner. He played semi-pro baseball for a couple of years after college until a shoulder injury derailed his baseball plans. He's a couple of years my senior, smart as a whip and an instantly likeable guy.

I call Roger and we all meet the following day. Pete repeats his demonstration and if anything, it's even more impressive. The core principle of his technology is using air to create an environment where the rock actually pulverizes itself. Pete believes it has the potential to revolutionize the mining industry.

Both Roger and Pete are effusive in their appraisal of the technology and are convinced it can revolutionize the hard rock gold mining industry. We sit down and began discussing how Pete sees the business structure of his company, named IMMCO, which stands for Industrial and Mining Machinery Company. We all agree to get together the following week.

The following day on Friday, I return to the office to share the experience with my partners. Phil asks me to step outside for a few minutes. He has a sheepish look on his face and appears totally embarrassed.

He tells me that Carl Anderson has given him an ultimatum and he doesn't know what to do. Carl told him that if he couldn't be the President of FSU, then both he and Joe would leave, taking all of our sales people along with him and start another company.

We both know if this were to happen, it will destroy FSU.

7 | IMMCO

Have you ever felt like a bucket of ice water has just been thrown in your face? When Phil tells me about Carl's ultimatum, that's exactly how I feel. My first instinct is to tell Carl to go screw himself. After all, FSU is my brainchild and there's no way I can work under Carl's arrogance and self-importance.

I know, however, that if most of our 15 registered reps leave with Carl, there's no way we can pay the rent and the staff overhead we've created. This a hell of a conundrum. I'm at a loss what to do. I tell Phil I'll think about it and ask him to tell Carl and Joe that we'll have an FSU company board meeting the following Monday at 6:00 p.m. to discuss the issues.

When I get home, I tell Jeannie about Carl's ultimatum and she's both apprehensive and supportive. I know that whatever I decide, our lives are in for a major change.

I call Roger Quast that evening and tell him what just happened. He says he has some stuff he wants to share and suggests we get together so we can talk over my situation.

We meet Saturday morning at Coco's restaurant and discuss both my current dilemma and the amazing demonstration we saw a couple of days earlier. Roger says he's been researching the potential for the rock-crushing technology. He feels that if it's structured properly, it has a good chance to make a lot of money as a securities play. I agree to call Pete Francis and suggest we all meet the following Monday morning.

By Monday afternoon, we've worked out a plan of action. Pete wants to establish a manufacturing operation in mining country. He has his eye on a 10-acre parcel just outside of Reno, Nevada that'll be an ideal manufacturing site. Pete knows he needs help and offers both Roger and me a significant minority stock position in IMMCO if we'll agree to obtain the financing and join him in his new company.

Pete will oversee design and manufacturing; Roger will be in charge of sales and I'll be in charge of company administration. We create a proposed timeline and budget and shake hands. We're all excited to be on a new adventure, this time in Nevada.

Monday evening, Phil, Carl, Joe and I all have our "Come-to-Jesus" board meeting. It's business-like and without animosity. In exchange for an agreed upon payment, I'll return my stock in FSU and resign, effective the last day of January, 1973.

Roger takes care of incorporating IMMCO in Nevada and we issue the stock. Pete is the majority shareholder and Roger and I take substantial minority stock positions. We offer insider-stock investment opportunities to several of the sophisticated investors we know and the initial funding is quickly completed.

We purchase the 10-acre parcel Pete has identified. Pete and his wife Sue lease an apartment and Pete starts acquiring the equipment we need to begin manufacturing operations.

Roger and his wife move to Reno. I lease a home in Virginia Foothills, a Reno suburb a couple of miles from our new manufacturing plant. Jeannie, her 3 children and I move to Nevada and IMMCO begins operations in Reno mid-February 1973. Our new adventure has begun.

The next year flies by quickly. Pete is a trained engineer and designs plans for four different size mills, ranging from 500 pounds to 20 tons of ore per hour. Sales are good and the reception for the IMMCO mills by the mining industry is positive. We sell enough mills to cover overhead and make a small profit.

We begin to see a niche where our mills have a distinct advantage. They're able to re-process ore tailings that have been mined decades before by mining equipment of the past century, quickly and much finer, releasing the fine gold and other minerals that remain in the ore.

This is an additional, collateral opportunity. Pete, Roger and I form an entity to take advantage of this discovery and call it First United Venture Mining, or FUVM. We offer the IMMCO shareholders an opportunity to participate financially and several of them become fellow shareholders. The timing is incredible. The price of gold is no longer pegged by the government at $35 per ounce, but is now allowed to float.

The gold standard was lifted on August 15, 1971 and gold is now trading at $120 per ounce, moving higher each month. With the increasing price of gold, our mills just might be the key to extracting some serious dollars from some of those old, shuttered gold mines.

An unmarried geologist in his 50's named Frank loves our IMMCO mills and starts hanging around the plant on a regular basis. We tell him of our plan to re-process tailings and he immediately turns us on to several long-shuttered mines he thinks have the potential to be very profitable. We put mills and the other equipment needed at a couple of old Nevada gold mines, hire a few men and begin processing gold tailings. Although we produce and sell several hundred ounces of gold, revenue barely covers the cost of operations.

However, we learn there's a problem brewing in paradise. Pete is a closet alcoholic. He's good at disguising his addiction for quite a while, but after a few months, it becomes worse and more noticeable. He begins coming into the office later and later in the morning, frequently slurring his words and getting belligerent with Roger and me. We talk with Pete about the issue to no avail. He's quickly becoming a liability to IMMCO rather than an asset.

After a particularly rancorous occurrence, Pete says, "Why don't you guys just buy me out? Sue and I would rather be in Florida. I'll give all my stock back to you guys for $15,000".

Yikes! We ask Pete to reconsider, but the next day he says he still wants out. This is a major, unplanned change in our plans. We have an extremely competent foreman named Russ to manage the manufacturing process, but we're still a small company of a dozen people and rely upon Pete for direction. A couple of days later, Pete signs over all of his stock, cashes the $15,000 check and beats it out of Nevada.

Roger and I are now the owners and majority shareholders in both IMMCO and FUVM.

This really puts IMMCO in a financial bind. We've removed a big chunk of the company's liquidity and realize that we'll have to find additional money somewhere if we're to continue operations.

A dentist in Las Vegas, Dr. Meierhenry, has heard of the IMMCO technology. He wants to become financially involved in IMMCO and pours $75,000 into the company for a substantial stock position.

He moves Dan Bode, a late 20's-something assistant to Reno as financial controller, and insists on having two directors on the company board. We agree, and ask our geologist, Frank, and IMMCO foreman, Russ, to serve on the Board of Directors along with Roger and me, assuring us control of the company.

Because we're totally open about our activities in FUVM, Dan Bode decides that they need a man on the ground to monitor our activities in that area. Dan asks if I know anyone that they might be able hire, and I think of Dick Parsons, the old friend that sheltered me when my marriage to Donna fell apart.

Dick is single and always looking for some excitement. I tell Dick about it, and he thinks it'll be a great adventure. He interviews with Dr. Meierhenry and Dan Bode and gets the job.

We are naïve. What we don't know is that when Dr. Meierhenry makes his investment, he's fronting for a Las Vegas Mafioso-type group complete with attorneys and enforcers on salary. They intend to obtain the IMMCO mill technology for themselves and the first step is to get rid of Roger and me.

Within two months, the new investor group calls for an IMMCO Board of Directors meeting at the local

Holiday Inn. We have no idea what we're walking into. They've sent Russ out of state on a pretense and won't allow him to return.

Roger, Frank and I get to the meeting room a half hour early. Shortly thereafter a group of six men appear.

The two new directors are joined by two attorneys, a big rough six foot two red-headed protector and a suave guy with slicked-back black hair and shoulder holster that's briefly visible as he adjusts his coat. To say we're nervous is the understatement of the year.

Although I've become the company president after Pete leaves, one of the attorneys immediately takes control. He says the first order of business is to terminate both Roger and me as IMMCO employees. The vote is three to two for our removal.

Frank has been bought off and votes against us. Roger and I are both shocked and devastated and leave the room.

When I get home, I tell Jeannie what just happened. Although I still own shares of our mining company, I have no source of income. There's nothing left for me in Reno, and I still have to figure out what is to become of FUVM. I load our personal effects in a trailer and Jeannie and the kids go back to North San Diego County so she can find a job.

I must now pick up the pieces of my life that are scattered about like the mine tailings we're mining.

56

8 | The Vega Mine

At the IMMCO plant in late 1975, we meet a couple of interesting visitors from Provo Utah. A financial planner named Glenn Pinegar and his side-kick Ted Lofgren have driven down to Reno to take a look at our mills. They're both Mormons and have a huge interest in the mining business. They aren't interested in actually mining themselves, but are looking for an investment they can offer their clients.

They love the IMMCO mills. Soon the conversation moves on to FUVM, our mining company, and our focus on re-processing old gold mine tailings. They know what's going on with gold prices and are determined to find a way to get involved.

Coincidently, we've just completed an agreement with Jim Valentine, an inveterate gambler living in Las Vegas who lost both his home and auto repaying casino gambling debts. He inherited several old family mining claims just across the Nevada border in California, about 60 miles from Las Vegas.

The mine is named the Vega. The mine produced a large quantity of gold and copper ore 50 years before. Jim's willing to sign the claims over to us in exchange for a couple thousand dollars.

We send Frank, our geologist, to thoroughly investigate the Vega mine tailings. He completes lots of sample assays from the tailing piles and the ore averages

2 to 3 percent copper and a quarter ounce of gold per ton. Frank says that although the gold is very fine, he's sure our IMMCO mills can profitably process the huge piles of mine tailings. We sign an agreement, hand Jim Valentine a check, and assume ownership of the mining claims.

The mine site is at the end of a 15-mile dirt road that snakes through the desert and up into the hills, where the mine is located. The road is abysmal, cut by washes and littered with small boulders. We clean up the road well enough to be passable and move a used 10' wide, 50' long mobile home onto the property so we'll have a place to stay.

Glenn and Ted want a piece of the Vega mine action. They agree to put up enough money to purchase a 5-ton IMMCO mill, a used 60Kw Buda generator, dump truck and all of the ancillary equipment we need to put the property into operation.

However, FUVM needs operating capital. I call Sydney Gordon, an attorney friend in Los Angeles, and ask if he has any ideas that might help us.

He introduces me to Bobby Frenkel, an Israeli with American citizenship. Bobby is exceptionally smart and agrees to put up the operating capital in exchange for partial ownership of FUVM. We transfer the stock and FUVM is ready to operate the property the week before the infamous Board of Directors meeting.

After Roger and I participate in that fateful meeting and Jeannie is safely back in California, Bobbie, Roger and I move into the mobile home at the Vega to complete the process of starting up the Vega mine.

Meanwhile, Dick Parsons is dispatched by the Meierhenry group to monitor the Vega property.

Dick rents a room at Whiskey Pete's hotel and casino at the Nevada state line and awaits orders from the Meierhenry group.

On Monday morning as we're starting our day at the Vega mine, we see a column of dust coming up the road. It's two sheriff's cars. The sheriffs tell Bobbie and me that they've been sent to enforce an eviction notice. The order states that we have to leave the Vega mine property immediately and they hand Bobbie a stack of papers. We have absolutely no idea what it's about.

Apparently, the Meierhenry group wants all of the equipment that FUVM has acquired as well as taking over IMMCO.

They've paid off Jim Valentine.

He files a complaint stating that we established our mill on property that actually belongs to him. The Meierhenry group is using the lawyers they have on salary and told him they'll pay for all legal expenses. Jim alleges that the FUVM agreement we have with him refers to a claim that is actually a couple of hundred feet away. He claims we've placed all of our equipment on his property, and not on the claims that he sold us.

The Meierhenry attorneys are using the courts as their weapon. We're forced to pack up our clothes, get into our vehicles and drive away. We find a motel in Henderson, Nevada to wait out the legal proceedings. Meanwhile, Roger is tired of the whole mess. He resigns, signs over all of his FUVM shares, and leaves for greener pastures.

Bobbie immediately drives the complaint down to our mutual attorney friend, Sydney Gordon. Sydney takes a look at the complaint and tells Bobbie it's pure bullshit, and immediately files a response to get the bogus complaint thrown out.

While this was going on, as president of FUVM, I receive a summons to sit for a deposition with the Meierhenry attorneys. I drive into Las Vegas by myself and enter an upper floor of legal offices in an office building on Las Vegas Boulevard. I'm ushered into a windowless room to join two attorneys and a court reporter.

I'm questioned for four or five hours and answer every question truthfully, resulting in a deposition transcript printed on a stack of paper two and a half inches thick.

However, because of the court calendar, it takes two weeks to get a court date. The following Friday the judge throws out the court eviction order. We again return to the property to get things started up again.

On Monday, we're presented with another complaint alleging the same charge. We're again ushered off of the property and I receive another deposition notice by the Meierhenry lawyers. I again speak the truth for another three or four hours, resulting in a second deposition transcript just over two inches thick.

Two weeks later, the same scene repeats itself. It becomes a process of two weeks on followed by two weeks off. Again, the sheriff appears on Monday. We have to leave the property for another two weeks, until the case can be heard by the court. And, I receive another deposition notice from the Meierhenry attorneys.

This time my third deposition is slightly over two and a half hours long and the transcript reporting that disposition somewhat slightly shorter.

I end up giving three separate depositions totaling more than 10 hours of questioning over the course of a month. When the deposition transcripts are stacked on top of one another, the end result is well over six inches of paper with testimony that all sounds the same. If you read one of them, you've read all of them.

The attorneys have tried their best to find incriminating evidence but end up with nothing more than a handful of dust. The lesson to be learned from this experience is to always tell the truth. When you tell the truth, you don't ever have to remember what you said before.

It's apparent that these guys aren't going to go away. After their third lawsuit attempting to remove us from the property is again dismissed on yet another Friday afternoon, we decide to remove our equipment from the Vega mine site.

I agree with Bobby to stay on the Vega property that night to keep an eye on things while Bobbie makes arrangements for us to stage our strategic retreat.

The Vega mine is in a really remote location. In addition to 15 miles of barely-passable dirt road, there are no utilities. The mobile home sits on a small knoll a couple hundred feet from the mill site with a view of the dirt road for at least a dozen miles. The only light at night other than the stars and moon is provided by 3 or 4 kerosene lanterns.

The closest human being is over 20 miles away.

Needless to say, once the sun goes down, the desert is pitch black. I can see down the hill and all the way across the valley for 25 miles and not a single light is visible. There's nothing to do except read an old paperback Louis L'Amour western novel for an hour or so by the light of a lantern. I hit the sack about 8:30 p.m.

An hour after I've fallen asleep, I'm abruptly shaken awake.

Literally.

Dick Parsons is standing over my bed. I ask him "What the hell are you doing here?".

He says, "I've been down at the bar at Whiskey Petes and Big Red is down at the bar getting roaring drunk. I came up to warn you that Big Red is telling everybody that he's going to drive up to the Vega mine and mess you up real good".

I know he's talking about Meierhenry's big red-headed enforcer. Dick tells me that he left the bar early and is taking the chance to drive out and warn me. He then turns around and leaves.

As I watch him drive back down the hill, I have to figure out how I'm going to stay alive and in one piece. My stomach feels like it's tied in a tight knot and filled with lead.

I decide if there's going to be trouble, I'm not willing to be the one going down. I fill all four kerosene lanterns, light and turn them up as high as possible. I place one lantern just outside the front door and scatter the remaining lanterns around the perimeter. I pick up the 16-gauge double barreled shotgun and load shells in the chamber.

Taking the safety off, I sit down on a folding chair in the darkness just inside the mobile home door.

Then I wait.

I have a great view from that front door. After about an hour and a half, in the distance a single, solitary light appears in the blackness, miles away. I watch as the light turns into headlights and bounces and winds its way up the dirt road towards me.

My apprehension mounts, in part because the road dips down into a wash and makes a curve around a small hill about a mile away. Approaching vehicles are briefly hidden out of sight until they're about a half mile away. I watch as the headlights swing down into the wash and I get mentally prepared for whatever is going to happen.

However, the headlights don't reappear out of that wash. I wait and wait, and my concern becomes almost tangible as the minutes stretch into hours. My anxiety intensifies as I imagine that Big Red has parked his car out of sight and is going to try and sneak up on me unseen. I remain awake, alert and nervous for hours, until sometime after 4:00 a.m.

After a cramped three or four hours in that chair, I decide Big Red must have had a change of heart. After all, in the midst of that pitch blackness, the lanterns are lighting up the area around the mobile home like New York's Times Square. It must have been apparent to him there won't be an element of surprise tonight. I never did see that car go back down the hill.

Shaken, I spent Saturday night back at the motel in Henderson.

However, the real action starts shortly after 4:00 a.m. Sunday morning. We've decided that in order to protect our equipment at the Vega, it all needs to be moved. At 5:00 a.m. we meet a mobile home mover and two 40' flatbed trucks, one pulling a big fork lift, at the intersection of I-15 and Nippon Road. By 6:00 a.m. Sunday morning, we pull onto the Vega mine site, break out the cutting torch and proceed to dismantle the entire mill site. The mobile home is soon hooked up and makes its way back to Las Vegas.

As we finish cutting the equipment loose and loading the flatbeds, Jim Valentine appears with two sheriff deputies. He demands they stop us immediately, saying we're taking equipment off of his property. Told by the sheriffs that it's a civil matter and that they can't get involved, he leaves.

We continue loading the flatbeds to the gills with everything they can hold. The Vega mine operation is over. All of our mining equipment is hauled down to Henderson, where we've made preparations to store it. The trucks are unloaded and everything will be safe until we need it again.

9 | Bud

Once we've removed all of our equipment from the Vega mine, there's no more reason for the Meierhenry group to continue their legal actions. Like a morning mist as the sun rises, they disappear and are never heard from again. We have enough mining equipment to set-up a decent hard rock mining operation stored in Henderson. Bobbie Frenkel and I decide to see if we can identify another opportunity to put it to work.

Over the next 4 or 5 months we visit a number of mining claims in Nevada and California. Some of them are extremely interesting, but it seems that each property we look at presents one or more problems that are preventing the properties from being operated.

We meet an old mining engineer who tells us about an incredible silver mine about 25 miles from Elko, Nevada in the Ruby Mountains. He offers to take us there. Piling into an old Jeep, we drive up a streambed strewn with huge boulders. It takes over two hours to drive less than a dozen miles, and we're glad to finally get out of that bouncing Jeep.

The engineer takes us over to a mine opening that leads into a maze of winding tunnels and big open stoped areas. We walk into the mine opening and turn on our helmet lights. The walls of the tunnels and the columns holding up the roof are shining with a dull silver glow as our lights strike them. The tunnels follow a four to five-foot thick band of solid galena ore.

Galena ore is an amalgamation of silver, lead, and zinc metals, and the sight is mesmerizing.

Water drips down from the roof, and rivulets run underfoot. The sight is almost beyond imagination. The ore all around us contains hundreds of ounces of silver per ton. We can only imagine the wealth all around us. That is, if a person can legally mine it.

The mining engineer tells us the story.

The mine was operated with Chinese miners around the turn of the 20th century. Because the mine is located at an elevation of 8,000 feet and virtually inaccessible, the mine was only worked about five months a year. The miners hauled solid metal ore out of the mountains to a smelter on the backs of mules to a railhead about 15 miles away.

During the winter the snow was so deep that the miners built tunnels under the snow pack from their shacks to the mine entrance. Because of the elevation and depth of the winter snow, the work was brutal.

However, legal problems regarding ownership stopped the mining operation completely in the early 1920's. The many intertwined lawsuits spanning many decades make a clear title impossible. The engineer said it'll undoubtedly take a team of lawyers years to clear the title. This sounds like a legal nightmare.

We aren't interested.

Toward the end of this period, I have a memorable experience and meet a man I'll never forget. His name is Bud Higgenbothem.

Bobbie, Morris Gordon, the father of our attorney Sidney Gordon, and I take a trip to the southern Sierra Nevada mountains area. We've been told that there's an old miner in Maricopa that knows every single mine in the area.

We're told he's 94 years old and lives alone in a tri-plex on the highway east of town. We find the only triplex on the highway, but don't know which unit he might be living in. I expect to find someone old, wrinkled and barely able to walk.

As I walk up to the building, I see a 10-speed bicycle leaning up against the railing of a small front porch. Through an open door I see a guy sitting at a kitchen table eating a bowl of cereal. I knock on the door jamb and ask if he knows where Bud Higgenbothem lives. He looks at me warily and asks why I want to know.

I tell him that we've been told Bud is the most knowledgeable miner in the area and we want to speak with him. His eyes twinkle, he bounds up out of his chair and quickly walks over to me with his hand extended. He says, "I'm Bud Higgenbothem." He wants to know if we'd come by earlier in the morning, because he's just come back from a 25-mile bike ride.

Once we'd exchange pleasantries, I introduce Bud to Bobby and Morris. Bud tells us he knows of a property that has enormous opportunity that he thinks might be available. He insists on driving there to show it to us.

He takes us around to the back of his apartment and the only vehicle in sight is an early 1950's Studebaker pickup truck with faded paint. Bud jumps into the driver's seat. However, the pickup won't start.

Bud opens up the hood and switches a couple of sparkplug wires around. He takes off the air filter and gets back in the pickup and turns the key.

Flames shoot up as the engine backfires out of the carburetor. Bud replaces the wires, the truck starts up right away, and he tells us to jump in. I stand up in the bed of the truck, holding onto the roof of the truck cab and we head out of town.

He points to a dirt road zig-zagging up the side of a steep mountain and says, "That's where we're going". The dozen or two hair-pins up the side of that steep mountain are tight enough to glue your butt-cheeks together.

When we finally arrive at the top of the switchbacks, Bud jumps out of the pickup and starts bounding up the side of the mountain. I follow him as closely as I can. I sure as hell can't let a 94-year old man out-hike me! Although a vein of high-grade silver ore has broken through to the surface, this isn't a property we're prepared to work.

On the way back down the hill, Bud tells us that if he was only 10 years younger, he'd love to go into the mining business with us. I do a quick mental calculation and figure that'd make him 84 years old. I shake my head in disbelief and ask Bud how he maintains such incredible physical shape. He relates that he's spent over 50 years working mines in the area, and only stopped when people told him he was too old to work.

It turns out his wife passed away about 5 years earlier. Bud said he was despondent for a while, then decided to start running to stay in shape. When he noticed he was getting winded a little earlier, he switched to riding a bicycle up and down the foothills of the Sierra Nevada mountains.

He tells us he got up before dawn the previous Saturday and did a 75-mile circuit on his bike around the Mariposa area. Bud said that he got back home he was a little tired and rested for a couple of hours. He says that later that night, he went out dancing with the ladies at the Senior Center. He says he likes to do it because there are more widow ladies wanting to dance then there are available men.

Bud Hickenbothem is definitely one of the most unforgettable characters I've ever met in my life. I'm sure I'll never forget him.

A couple of weeks later, I have an epiphany which comes about in a totally unintended manner. Bobbie's on the phone, speaking with a guy about all of the capabilities we have in FUVM. He's exaggerating to such an extent that it makes me almost embarrassed to be listening to the conversation. When he hangs up, I ask him why he was feeding this guy such a line of bullshit.

Bobbie looks at me and says, "I don't mind lying to anyone. The only people I won't lie to are family and friends."

All of a sudden, I get a cold feeling in my middle. A huge red flag is waving in front of me. I know if what he's telling me is true, I'm in deep trouble. I'm a business partner and definitely neither family nor friend.

Shortly thereafter, I tell Bobbie that I'm ready to throw in the towel. I sign my FUVM stock certificates and tell him all of the equipment now stored in Henderson belongs to him.

I have neither an automobile nor place to live, and precious few dollars. I decide that I'll head back to North San Diego County. Maybe I can hook up again with Jeannie and the kids. I know I'll find a way to make a living.

10 | DFS

One of the most important necessities in the lives of Californians is mobility.

Stuck in Los Angeles, I find an old beater that'll get me around for a couple hundred dollars. I drive down to Oceanside and decide to stop by FSU, my old financial planning company to see how they're doing.

I'm totally mystified to find the FSU suite in the office building I'd built is vacant. I look in the phone book and find there's no listing for the company, either. FSU apparently no longer exists. I wonder to myself, what the heck happened?

I find my old partner Phil Jauregui's home phone number in the phone book and give him a call that evening. He begins the conversation by telling me he's really sorry.

He tells me he sincerely apologizes for the way I'd been forced out of FSU. He says he didn't know what to do at the time and would have done things much differently if a do-over was possible. Phil then tells me how it all came down.

He tells me that when I left FSU, Carl Anderson got his coveted position as company president. Phil said Carl took over my role as presenter in the financial planning seminars, but he wasn't very effective. His inflated ego apparently rubbed people the wrong way, leading to fewer seminar attendees becoming clients of the firm.

Phil says that in less than six months, he and Carl had a knock-down, drag-out brawl. He says there was no way he could continue to work with Carl and it was a huge relief when Carl and Joe Vosmik both resigned and left the company.

Phil tells me he was looking for a new start, so he closed down FSU and started a new financial planning company he named Diversified Financial Systems, or DFS for short. He hired a few financial planners and took over the remaining FSU real estate investment partnerships until they were all liquidated at a profit.

He built another, larger office building a couple of blocks north of the old office on El Camino Real in Oceanside and hired another management team. Phil says he's in the process of expanding his business and asks me if I'll forgive him for the past and come back to work with him.

Phil tells me he really wants me to again be the presenter at the financial planning seminars. He offers to pay me a salary plus an override on sales if I'll become DFS's Vice President in charge of hiring and training.

Now at age 36, broke and without a place to live, I tell him I'm willing to return as an employee. I tell Phil that before I can accept his offer, he needs to understand my present personal and financial situation. He listens intently and says he has a possible solution.

Phil tells me that he just purchased a home as an investment at 1615 N Meyers St in Oceanside. The home is literally one block from the beach. He says it's empty without any furniture, but I'm welcome to spend a few nights there while I figure out what I'm going to do. I agree to accept his offer.

The home's about 30 years old. It has a large family room in the back of the house alongside a single-car garage which opens onto an alley at the rear of the home. After a couple of days, I make an offer to Phil.

In exchange for free rent, I'll remodel his home for him. I plan to combine the family room and garage and turn it into a one-bedroom apartment with its own separate entrance to the street. I've figured out how I can convert the large storage closet into a small kitchen. That way he'll own a 3-bedroom home with an additional attached one-bedroom apartment.

Phil's enthusiastic about the idea because it'll significantly increase the value of his investment. The upside for me is that I'll have a free place to live for a while. Phil agrees to pay for the materials, and I complete the entire remodel in about a month.

Over the following several months, I wake up around dawn each morning for a refreshing 2-mile run on the beach. Life is again becoming good.

I resume my work as a financial planner and again begin presenting the financial planning seminars. I hire and train at least a dozen bright young men as financial planners over the next few months. With practically no personal overhead, I'm able to save most of the money I make. I lease a new Mercedes 240 and start looking for a home or condo of my own to buy.

Within months I find a condo development under construction in Solana Beach overlooking the Del Mar racetrack. I'm able to purchase a brand-new 3-bedroom condo at 323 Shoemaker Lane for $85,000. During this time, Jeannie and I speak several times and we decide to get back together and see if we can make our relationship work. Although we've been living separately for over a year, we're still legally married.

Jeannie and her 3 children move into the condo with me right after construction's completed and the escrow closed. Light and airy, the condo is perfectly situated on the hillside above the racetrack with a partial view of the ocean. With high ceilings and walls of glass, this condo is sure to be a wonderful investment. I live there for two years and enjoy every day.

Although I'm making good money, I begin to get concerned about the way things are going at DFS. Phil has started selling sub-ordinated trust deed investments paying ten percent interest to his clients, and using the money to buy personal real estate investments.

Although property values are still going through the roof in North San Diego, I know he's playing with dynamite and speculating in a big way. More importantly, it's also probably not legal.

I recall a vivid dream I have one night involving Phil. In my dream he's constructing a large building that requires a heavy foundation containing many pieces of iron rebar. In my dream, he's trying to get by with less than half the number of rows of rebar, and I'm trying to help him. I'm wearing a three-piece suit and dress shoes, pushing wheel barrow loads of concrete over planks to fill the footings before the inspector comes around.

I remember telling Phil that there's no way he's going get it done before the inspector arrives.

That dream haunts me for months.

I continue to advertise for, hire, and train new financial planning advisors and DFS prospers. One of the young men that comes by is Dan Pulvers. Dan is a Dartmouth University grad about 10 years my junior with an existing real estate sales license. He's extremely bright and sucks up all the information he receives.

Another is a young man with a slight stuttering impairment named Terry Brazzell. Terry has been working for a personal development guru and wants to learn how to make $100,000 a year. I like him and hire Terry just before Christmas 1976. I personally guarantee a small loan from DFS to help get him and his family through the holidays.

Both men obtain their insurance and securities licenses and are dedicated to the business. Real estate investments have been performing extremely well as home prices continue to increase. In 1978 alone, single family home values in the town of Encinitas shoot up over twenty percent. It's hard to lose money investing in real estate in North San Diego County these days.

The following year I sell the Shoemaker condo for almost twice the price I'd paid for it and move into a home in Cardiff. Although I don't know it at the time, forty years later that same condo is resold for ten times the amount I sell it for.

However, my personal life is again in the throes of change. Jeannie and I don't fight or have arguments, but it's becoming obvious that love has gone out of our relationship. In 1978 we agree to an amicable divorce and go our separate ways.

That vivid dream I had regarding Phil, however, continues to haunt me. I just can't shake the feeling that it's time for me to move on.

I tell Phil that I'm going to resign from DFS and start looking for a small office. When Dan Pulvers and Terry Brazzell learn that I'm leaving the company, they tell me they want to join me in my new endeavor.

I'm willing to allow them to come with me and Phil gives the whole idea his blessing. I give them each a small equity interest in the company I name Creative Financial Planning. After a short time, I sign a year lease on a small office space in San Marcos, buy office furniture and order phones to be installed.

It's now the fall of 1978, and now almost 38 years old, I begin another new adventure.

11 | CFP

Ah, the heady days of beginning another adventure. So many details are involved in starting a new business it can become mind boggling.

The first couple of weeks of Creative Financial Planning's existence are pretty hectic. A new corporate entity must be formed. Creating a relationship with an NASD Broker-Dealer and establishing General Agent relationships with multiple insurance companies are both crucial.

And the physical logistics: desks and office equipment to be set up, supplies purchased, business cards and letterhead designed and printed. Last but not least, a brand-new set of acetates must be created for the financial planning seminars to come.

Terry Brazzell, Dan Pulvers and I set up our individual and company game plan. Dan's primary responsibility is to identify real estate investment opportunities appropriate for creating limited partnerships for our clients. Terry is charged with following up with potential future clients. I'm pegged to make arrangements for venues to hold and deliver the financial planning seminars, in addition to managing my own existing client accounts.

I'm again single, so 12 to 14-hour days for me are the norm. The first few months fly by quickly and the company begins to prosper. Soon it becomes apparent that Terry's heart isn't in the business. He's become disengaged in our weekly meetings and is scheduling fewer client interviews. It isn't long before he offers to sell his interest in CFP for $8,000. We agree to buy him out, and he takes his money and runs.

We acquire several promising real estate investment opportunities, create limited partnerships, and the partnerships sell out quickly. Interest rates are going up rapidly, but we're still confident that real estate prices will continue to increase in North San Diego county. Two additional financial planners soon join CFP and our small office is bursting at the seams.

During the summer of 1979 I receive a phone call from my old Los Angeles attorney friend, Sydney Gordon. A CPA friend of his just told him he has a client that's looking to fund a unique investment opportunity and Sydney thinks I might be able to help him out. I arrange to meet with Zachary Taylor, president of a company called G-Force Productions at our offices in San Marcos along with his sidekick, Tyk Phillips.

After a short time, it's apparent Zachary and I share a very similar upbringing and we hit it off right away. He wants to raise $10 million for a multi-media road production called "Elvis: The Final Tribute". He intends to take a road production show around the world combining vintage, unseen video footage of Elvis and state-of-the-art sound, laser and special effects.

I decide to help him and personally arrange for a limited partnership agreement to be prepared. Although that project never gets off of the ground, we become close friends and remain so to this day.

Meanwhile, Dan discovers a brand-new office complex in the completion stage in San Marcos. The location is ideal, right off of the freeway and I sign a lease for three thousand square feet. We order the interior build-out to our specifications and prepare to move our office.

Dan and I know that if the company is to grow rapidly, we'll have to offer equity positions to the top financial planners. We bring in Ken Williams from Orange County, Jim Stewart from Rancho Bernardo, and add Chet Niebrugge CPA, as our financial controller. All of them become minority shareholders and the company grows rapidly.

Money is good. I buy a 1959 Mercedes 300SL roadster convertible and drive the wheels off as my primary transportation. I buy a second home at Lake Tahoe, in Stateline Nevada. CFP opens a satellite office in South Lake Tahoe, and I hire two financial planners for that office. Before long, I'm splitting my time between offices. I begin spending half of each month in Lake Tahoe and the other half in San Diego county.

I conduct bi-weekly financial planning dinner seminars in Lake San Marcos and Mission Viejo in Orange County, and additional monthly seminars in South Lake Tahoe. The seminars typically range in size between 50 and 200 attendees.

Dan continues his real estate education and obtains the MAI designation, equivalent to a doctorate in real estate evaluation. We hire additional qualified financial planners and the business grows even more.

Between office staff and planners, our new office now numbers 18 people.

We establish a business relationship with a young real estate attorney, Jeff Cheyne, who oversees the legal aspects of each structured investment and drafts all of our legal documents. Over the following year, CFP continues to prosper.

We create over a dozen real estate limited partnerships in land development and commercial and residential construction projects. Some of the partnerships are very short-term investments and the properties are sold at a significant profit to both our partners and CFP. Others have a time-line of 3 to 5 years.

On May 18, 1980 I'm scheduled to attend a meeting of our national broker-dealer's principals in Seattle. I depart from San Diego Lindberg Field early in the morning. Ninety percent of the way to Seattle, the Captain gets on the intercom and says that he's just received an urgent message. He says that we've been re-routed 50 miles west because of a volcanic explosion that occurred a half-hour earlier.

He assures us that we're totally safe, and urges us to look out the right-side window of the airplane if we can. The volcano is Mt St. Helens. It just popped.

I'm sitting at the window on the right side of the plane and can't believe what I'm seeing. An enormous thick black column of smoke, dust and debris is rising through the cloud cover. It almost looks alive, and eventually rises 50,000 feet into the air until it's out of sight. We don't realize the enormity of the disaster until many hours later.

However, things in the financial world are unraveling throughout the country. In early 1980, the prime interest rate reaches 15%. Mortgage interest rates are even higher. The real estate developments that we've acquired and spent a lot of time and money developing aren't selling as quickly as planned.

We create a limited partnership to build three custom homes in a highly desirable part of San Marcos, designed by a top Del Mar architectural firm. These homes are absolutely stunning, but we can't find buyers.

It seems that nobody can afford a mortgage payment carrying an interest rate of 18% a year. I eventually lease one of the homes for 9 months in order to generate a minimal income to the partnership. Steve and Julie, my eldest children, move in with me.

Another partnership is a 37-acre prime residential parcel on the outskirts of Escondido that we subdivide and improve with roads and utilities. It's beautiful, but we simply can't find a buyer.

Two Orange County developers each tell us they love the property, but won't be able to buy it until interest rates come down. They urge us to hold onto the property until people can afford the mortgage payments on the homes they plan to build.

As we search for additional real estate, it becomes an almost impossible task for Dan to find genuine opportunities in our local real estate market. I begin researching additional investment opportunities that offer growth opportunities for our clients, rather than relying exclusively on real estate and the stock market.

During this time, my personal life is in limbo. One of my clients tells me about a psychic astrologer named Georgie Copeland living in a small town in central California. She says that Georgie comes down to San Diego regularly for readings and suggests perhaps I should schedule a meeting with her and ask her what she foresees.

Georgie combines astrology with card readings, and has been conducting personal readings for many clients in the San Diego area for years. I schedule an appointment with her to see what it's all about. Georgie gives me a reading and it's quite entertaining. I can't speak to its accuracy, but I like her and tell her I'll probably see her again.

Meanwhile, some of our limited partnerships are getting into trouble. We find ourselves borrowing money at interest rates as high as two percent per month. Nobody in their right mind ought to do that, but we're attempting everything we can think of to keep our partnerships afloat.

By mid-1981, the prime interest rate exceeds 17 percent and it becomes impossible to borrow money from any source. As a last resort, Chet starts making loans from partnerships that contain excess cash in their accounts to partnerships that are in trouble in order to keep them out of foreclosure.

Although the loans are fully documented and secured by notes, they aren't kosher. Our attorney has failed to disclose the intra-partnership loans to new clients.

In the fall of 1981, we hold a Board of Directors meeting of the five CFP shareholders. I insist that we discontinue creating new real estate limited partnerships until interest rates go down and the real estate market stabilizes.

I'm over-ruled by the other board members, who argue that we have to keep creating new partnerships to provide the cash flow the company is reliant on. They're right in their reasoning, but I tell them that I can't in good conscience keep promoting and selling something that I feel is going to blow up in our face.

They tell me, "This is the way it's going to be. If you don't like it you can leave".

I don't like it. I'm the largest shareholder, but no longer control CFP. I resign and tender my shares back to the company. Now I have to find something else to do.

12 | Georgie

My final months with CFP, I spend a lot of time researching other investment vehicles that may be available as options for our clients. One of the ventures that I previously heard about, but never got around to checking out, is an alternative energy company headquartered in Denver, Colorado.

An attorney/inventor is the president of the company. He's invented a method to take petroleum petcoke, the carbon-rich waste residue from crude oil refining commonly known as 'coke', and transform it into ethanol. He believes the ethanol he produces can be added to gasoline to reduce America's dependence on imported oil.

Petroleum coke looks like black cinders and is non-toxic. Literally millions of tons of this stuff are stored in piles surrounding refineries all around the United States. The economics are very good because coke is to be the feed stock and has minimal to no commercial value.

The principal in the company is Bill Kilpatrick. He's constructed a proof-of-concept machine to produce ethanol from petroleum coke in the Denver area. He has designed a tax-sheltered investment vehicle to raise enough capital to begin mass production of ethanol. I want to go there in person and check it out.

The timing appears to be perfect now.

I fly into the Denver Metro airport and land late in the year. Denver's in the midst of an early cold snap and everything I see is brown. And, it's bitterly cold. I can't imagine living here.

When I get to the outskirts of town, the operation comes into sight. The pilot machine is over 50 feet long and most impressive. The machine is fired up, petroleum coke is shoveled onto a conveyer belt in one end, and ethanol dribbles out of a tube at the other end. Impressive it is! It looks like this might be a significant part of a solution to bring the country some much-needed energy independence.

I go out to an early dinner with about a dozen people after an afternoon demonstration. Many of the people joining us are principals in small investment companies around the country. There I meet Al Folsom, a promoter who lives in the Denver area. We seem to hit it off.

Bill Kilpatrick's petroleum coke-to-ethanol project doesn't ever get off of the ground, in large part because the IRS disputes the tax structure of his offering. However, I stay in contact with Al Folsom because he tells me he's planning to take a new energy company public and thinks I might be able to help him.

When I return to San Diego, the client that introduced me to Georgie Copeland, the psychic astrologer, suggests I call her to see what she sees in the cards for me. I phone Georgie to see when she plans to be back in town. She tells me she'll be back in San Diego the following week and we schedule a reading.

Just before I leave my home for that reading, Al Folsom calls. He says that he's just leaving a business meeting in San Diego and would like to have dinner afterwards. I tell him about the reading I've scheduled, and he suggests that I bring Georgie along after my reading. I drive to meet Georgie for the reading and the only new thing she can tell me is that I have a huge amount of change taking place in my life at this time. That's not news to me.

After the reading, I tell Georgie about Al's offer to have her join us for dinner. She's staying at her mother's home and tells her mother that she'll be back home in a couple of hours. We meet Al at the Hilton hotel on San Diego Bay and all have a good time and a lively conversation.

After dinner and drinks, I take Georgie back to her mother's home. I drop her off about 10:30 p.m. and wait at the curb until she gets into the house. As she's walking toward the front door, she trips and I see her fall.

Just as I jump out of the car to run over to her, she gets up, tells me she's okay and goes inside. What I don't know is that when she fell, she fractured her hip.

The next day I call to see how she's doing. She tells me her hip hurts a lot and she scheduled a doctor appointment for later that afternoon. The following day I call and she tells me she's going to require surgery.

The doctor wants to do a hip replacement the following week. I'm devastated, and feel guilty for the whole incident. Especially so, because I know that she has rheumatoid arthritis and walks with a cane because of badly damaged knees.

When the surgeon examines her, he tells her that she's going to need a complete knee replacement in addition to a new hip if she ever wants to walk again. Although she's married, her husband is reluctant to drive down from their home in central California to see her. I visit her every day in the hospital after her surgery. She tells me that she's going to file for divorce and doesn't plan to go back to central California.

Meanwhile, Al Folsom calls. He wants me to become the director of financial public relations for Axaton, his new oil company. He offers me 50,000 shares of insider stock at a nickel a share plus a generous salary. He plans to do a public offering on the Vancouver stock exchange at fifty cents a share, and expects the price of the stock to go up rapidly.

I accept his offer, fly to Denver and lease a home in the neighboring town of Aurora. I begin putting the wheels in motion and prepare to move.

When I tell Georgie about the development, she states that she wants to join me in Colorado with her three children, none of whom I've ever met. If this isn't the last thing I ever expected, it can't be far from it. What do I say?

I think, what the hell. I'm single and I'm embarking on a new adventure. Why not give it a go? Even though I have reservations, I tell Georgie I'm willing to give it a try.

Georgie gives her nephew a list of all of her personal property at her home in central California. She gives him a key to the front door along with a letter giving him authority to act on her behalf. As it so happens, her husband is visiting friends in Southern California and the home is empty.

I lease a U-Haul truck, pick up her nephew and we drive to her vacant home. We begin loading all of her personal property for the drive to my new home in Aurora. As we're loading the truck, a neighbor comes by to see what's going on. Georgie's nephew shows him her letter of authorization and instructions and the neighbor goes home and immediately calls the police. When the police arrive, they decide it's a civil matter and leave.

Once we complete loading all the items on her list, I get in the truck and hit the road to Colorado. I keep looking in the rear-view mirror to see if any red and blue lights appear behind me until I'm all the way out of California. I drive straight through, stopping only for gas. I arrive at my new home in Aurora and unload the truck.

As soon as the rental truck is empty, I return it to U-Haul and fly back to San Diego. I learn that Georgie is scheduled to be released from the hospital the following day. I drive to the hospital the next morning and find that Georgie's in a full leg cast, doped up on pain medication, fortunately feeling minimal pain.

She wedges herself into the front passenger seat using pillows to support her leg. We drive over and I meet her three children for the first time and we all drive directly to Colorado.

I think to myself, am I being foolish or impulsive? I decide it's probably a fair amount of both.

The drive from San Diego is 1,100 miles and takes two days. The car is packed, with 13-year old Chuck, 11-year old Tiffeny and 9-year old John in the back seat and the trunk crammed with all their stuff. Georgie takes pain pills as prescribed and we make the transit without difficulty. When we arrive at our new home in Aurora, it's a huge relief to all of us.

At the time all of this is going down, I've been a practicing vegetarian for almost a year. I'll never forget the fun of trying to encourage three young children to enjoy a vegetarian meal.

After a few days and a dinner of steamed vegetables smothered in cheddar cheese over brown rice, the petite blond 11-year old Tiffeny pipes up and asks, "What's wrong with a good old pot roast now and then?". I decide she's right, and we eat a more balanced diet from that point forward.

13 | Chaos

My rash decision to embark on this new life adventure ushers a period of unmitigated chaos into my life. This messy period lasts six years and brings a tsunami of unsettled change.

Describing our first few weeks in Colorado as chaotic is definitely an understatement. I locate and purchase the many pieces of furniture we need, and now it's finally time to become acquainted. Actually, it's past time, but who's counting? I'm again 'dad' to another ready-made family, this time ages 13, 11 and 9.

They all need to be in school, so I have the responsibility of enrolling them. Georgie is healing from new hip and knee replacement surgeries and the healing process seems glacial. As she is also dealing with decades of rheumatoid arthritis, you can imagine how long it takes her to become even relatively mobile.

I finally have a chance to catch up on some of Georgie's history. Her eldest daughter Perri Williams, by her first husband, is living in San Diego. She's married with two young sons, Philip and Patrick. The three children with us, Chuck, Tiffeny and John are by her second husband, Cal Custer. She just left and is in the process of divorcing her third husband, David Copeland.

I'm the fourth man in her life. However, I figure her history can't be too bad because I'm on my own third relationship. As time goes by, her multiple surgeries heal and family life begins to even out.

Meanwhile, I'm settling into my new job as the director of public relations at Axaton. The company had a successful initial public offering on the Vancouver Stock Exchange and there're many public relations duties to attend to. My new office in Aurora, Colorado is busy.

Al Folsom is the prime promoter of Axaton. Ken is a young attorney and the company president, and Roy is the head geologist. It's my job to become familiar with all of the company's oil and gas prospects, prepare the annual SEC 10k financial report filing and be the liaison with the financial community.

Roy and I travel to many of Axaton's oil and gas leases and wells throughout Oklahoma, West Virginia and Pennsylvania. We visit quite a few tiny mountain towns in West Virginia and joke a lot about all of the homely waitresses we come across. I learn a hell of a lot in a very short period of time.

The months fly by, with daily calls from securities analysts and stock brokers. At the end of the fiscal year, I prepare the annual 10k financial report for the Securities Exchange Commission and distribute it to the financial community. During this time the company's stock increases in value. I'm able to sell blocks of my initial nickel-per-share insider stock at prices all the way up to $4.50 per share.

Once Axaton's first annual report has been filed, my responsibilities slow down. Al Folsom asks me if I'm willing to move back out west, as he is working on another company that he hopes to take public. After 14 months in Aurora, Colorado we leave for Scottsdale, Arizona. Georgie and I rent a 3-bedroom apartment a couple of blocks from Old Scottsdale. It's summertime, and it's bloody hot.

After a couple of weeks, we decide it's time to get married and formalize our relationship. We rent a marriage chapel on the Queen Mary in Long Beach, California, and with a small group of close friends, tie the knot. I'll never forget the musician nor his prescient choice of music. He asks, "Do you want me to play something traditional or contemporary?". I tell him I'd prefer something contemporary and he chooses, "New York, New York". The lyrics, "If I can make it here, I can make it anywhere" are spot on.

As it turns out, it'll take a better man than me to make this marriage work.

The company that Al Folsom is planning to do a public stock offering for never takes off and I'm again looking for a job. Al calls an old friend who runs a registered investment advisory service in Las Vegas. He tells his friend of my background and is told that there's a spot for me.

I drive to Las Vegas for an interview and am hired on the spot. I take and pass the NASD's Series 65 Registered Investment Advisor exam a couple of weeks later. I rent a studio apartment and travel back and forth weekly from Scottsdale to Las Vegas.

Not enjoying the office environment at all, I quit in the fall of 1982. I've only been there for about four months, and decide to go back to familiar territory in Southern California.

Two weeks later, Georgie, family and I move back to California. We find and lease a small home in El Segundo, California for a couple of years. I work at several jobs, but none of them provide anything I can get my teeth into. Our small home has a huge built-in bar-b-que and we spend many weekends barbequing and cooking with family and friends.

However, my most potent memory is waking up at 4:00 a.m. one Sunday morning with an insight on life, karma and my purpose on this planet.

Georgie and I have numerous ongoing disagreements regarding predestination versus free will. It creates a great deal of strain on our relationship. I believe each person is born with free will, with the ability to make their own personal decisions.

Georgie is a psychic astrologer. She believes that unless events in life are predestined to occur, the future predictions she gives her clients are impossible. My belief system and hers seem totally incompatible.

I can't find anything to write with or on, but locate an orange felt pen and write on the back of a calendar. It's like taking dictation. I fill the entire back of the calendar with text.

The voice that I clearly hear, states, "There has been disagreement between you as to whether predestination or free will is the operative force in the Universe. The truth is, both are."

The 'voice' goes on to state that our individual spirit chooses a family unit that will provide us with the opportunity to learn one or more lesson. It continues on to state that each of us is given the opportunity to choose a course of action in response to an event. That's where free will comes in.

Once we choose our course of action, the lesson we've chosen to learn is predetermined. This process occurs throughout life. If you don't learn the lesson you've chosen, you get the opportunity to experience that same lesson again until you learn it or die.

There's a lot more to it, but that's a subject for another discussion.

The Summer Olympic Games are held in Los Angeles that summer of 1984. I've remained close friends with Zachary Taylor over the previous five years and receive a phone call from him that spring.

Zachary tells me that his company, G-Force International Entertainment Corporation, has just signed a contract with the US Olympic Games Organizing Committee to create a memorable lighting display for the 1984 Olympics summer games. He asks if I'm available and interested in helping out.

Zachary plans to produce the biggest lighting event in the history of Los Angeles to celebrate the opening of the Games. He additionally plans to light the iconic Hollywood sign throughout the games. His plan is to position over 80 huge searchlights on the mountaintop overlooking the Hollywood sign and cover them with gels in the colors of the rings of the Olympics emblem.

My job is to monitor the searchlights during the opening ceremony as they rotate beams of color across the entire LA basin.

What a gas! The mountaintop above the Hollywood sign is a huge flat area. A tightly controlled restricted area, it houses all of Los Angeles' various law enforcement and security agencies emergency communications equipment. The 80 searchlights are brought up the mountainside and lined up side by side.

Each is topped with a gel in one of the colors of the Olympic rings and, at the designated time, simultaneously lit. They fill the sky over the entire LA basin with rotating color and the sight is awe-inspiring.

Simultaneously, Zachary positions individually controlled two-million watt light cannons below the iconic Hollywood sign. The letters of the sign are illuminated every evening throughout the Olympic Games. What an unforgettable experience!

During this time, Al Folsom remains in touch. He calls one day and asks me to do some research on the subject of financial privacy. Although I don't know it at the time, this phone call is the springboard to my next adventure.

Financial privacy involves the setting up of trusts in tax haven jurisdictions that have laws protecting the assets of wealthy individuals. This isn't done to avoid taxes, but to keep beneficial ownership of assets private. At this time the Bahamas, Cayman Islands, Monserrat and several other jurisdictions all have constitutions protecting businesses and trusts from requiring disclosure of beneficial ownership.

One of the people I learn a lot from is Ron Boutwell, a Mormon attorney about 10 years my senior. Ron is currently living in Las Vegas. He's studied personal financial privacy trusts for several years and willingly shares many ideas. He says that although literally trillions of dollars of assets are hidden around the world, the IRS, DOJ, and other government entities are making it more difficult to set up new offshore trusts.

He tells me that an international conference on financial privacy is taking place in New Orleans the following month and invites me to come along as his guest. I join him at the conference and come away deciding it isn't anything that I want to be involved with.

On the way home, Ron tells me that after attending the conference, he feels the same way. He says that the thing that interests him most is the development of the personal computer. By 1984, the IBM PC is a couple of years old and rapidly becoming widely accepted. He's interested in using that new technology to help automate medical offices.

I know next to nothing about computers and tell him so. However, Ron says, you know a lot about sales. He asks if I'll consider joining him in starting a medical office automation software company. Ron offers to provide the seed capital and says he'll pay me a livable salary.

I meet with him several times over the next months, and decide to join him in his new adventure as his vice president of sales. We all pack up and our family moves to Las Vegas.

Upon arriving in Las Vegas, we lease a 4-bedroom home with a swimming pool in the southeast part of town and I enroll the kids in their new schools. We then receive some unexpected news. Georgie's eldest daughter, Perri Williams, is filing for divorce and needs a place to live.

As it turns out, we're that place. Shortly after I sign the lease on our home, Perri and her two young sons move in with us. I now find myself responsible for the support of nine souls, including myself.

Shortly after Perri and the boys move in with us, Georgie tells me she thinks her name sounds too immature. I ask her what name she wants to be called and help her file a legal change of name. Thereafter, and forever more, she's known as Ashley.

Meanwhile, Ron incorporates our new business as MD Management Systems, Inc. We sign a contract to license a multi-user DOS based operating system from a company named Thoroughbred Software. We also contract with a company headquartered in Newport Beach, California to private license their medical office automation software program.

Equipment is purchased, employees hired, documentation and marketing materials printed, and we're in business. We begin exhibiting the MD Management Systems office automation system at medical conferences.

While the new business venture is taking off, things get even more crowded at home. Our home seems to be a magnet for unloved and/or unwanted children. One day the kids bring a teenage age boy about 15 years old home with them. His name is Doug Huffman. They found him living in a hole he dug in the desert and covered with an old piece of plywood. He really needs a bath and something to eat.

He receives both at our home.

The story is that he ran away from home because his step-mother didn't like his long hair and forced his father to cut it all completely off. He vows to never again talk with his family. I welcome him into our home and become his temporary 'dad'. He stays with us for six months, until I'm able to get him to call his parents around Christmastime. Soon thereafter he patches up his relationship with his parents and is reunited with his family.

About the same time, another couple of elementary school kids come to live with us. We learn that their parents have both lost their casino jobs. We meet their parents. They tell us they have to move out of the home they're renting and they ask if their children can stay with us until the current semester ends. They promise that it'll only be for five or six weeks. They end up staying with us for almost seven months.

Meanwhile, my personal finances are totally decimated. My old financial planning company, CFP, is in the throes of dissolving many of the real estate limited partnerships. As I had predicted, high interest rates have killed off any chance of profit. I determine that my only financial salvation is personal bankruptcy. Ron Boutwell prepares the paperwork and drives to court with me. I become legally bankrupt.

However, sometimes it doesn't just rain. It simply pours.

Two weeks later, a sheriff appears at my home and delivers a lawsuit filed by Michael Aguirre, a San Diego attorney. He represents a number of investors that participated in the real estate limited partnerships formed by CFP several years earlier.

Unfortunately, I have neither the money to offer a settlement nor money to hire a lawyer.

The lawsuit names me, the other principals of CFP and our real estate attorney, Jeff Cheyne. All of the other CFP principals are able to settle the lawsuit, so the only defendants remaining in the trial are Jeff Cheyne's attorneys and me.

I have to be my own attorney. I soon learn what it feels like to sit at the defense attorney's table in front of the judge. The trial takes an entire week. When the dust finally settles, my penalty is a $50,000 restitution judgment that will have to be paid in installments over time.

Meanwhile, over a period of 18-months, MD Management Systems has been successful in installing a couple of dozen medical office automation systems in California and Nevada. As we're making plans to exhibit the office automation system at a national medical conference, we receive a registered letter.

Unbeknown to us, another company has been selling medical office automation software for a year longer than us. The name of the company is MD Systems, Inc., based out of Woodland Hills, California. Their complaint states that the name of our business is too close to theirs.

They file an injunction preventing us from marketing any more software under the name of MD Management Systems, Inc. It's absolutely devastating. Ron says that the expense of re-incorporating the company under another name isn't in the cards and decides to fold the business.

For me, that means that a month before Christmas 1985, I'm again out of a job. There's nothing more keeping me in Las Vegas.

Once again, I decide to move back to California and find a way to support my huge acquired family.

14 | One Card

We arrive back in Southern California in December, a couple of weeks before Christmas. We don't have a place to live. I don't have a job and just barely enough money for a deposit and first month's rent on a house.

Within a day, I find a 3-bedroom home in Encino that meets our needs. The owners of the home, who have built another home a couple of blocks away, take pity on us and lease us their old home. Now I've got to find a way to bring in some money.

I scour the want ads in the LA Times and interview for several jobs, none of which pan out. After a week of beating my head against a wall, I finally I see an ad that looks like it's directed to me.

The ad states that a new company called One Card International is looking for four people to assist them in raising seed capital. The company is founded by Dr. Melvin Salvorson, the inventor of the Visa and Mastercard credit card programs years earlier. He intends to issue a single card that will be tied to all of your existing credit cards, including your AmEx card. That way, you'll only have to carry a single credit card instead of a wallet full of credit cards.

His intent is to also encode your medical records on the card. Your medical records will only be accessible by special terminals located in doctor's offices. That way no matter where you are, in the case of an emergency a treating physician will have your health records immediately available to them.

The investor segment that they intend to reach to fund this new company are physicians throughout Southern California. They plan to ultimately take One Card International public, making this an excellent ground floor investment opportunity for doctors.

I arrive at the small office where they're conducting interviews of prospective employees. I'm dismayed to see the room literally jammed with young men who arrived there before me. At the ripe old age of 45, I appear to be at least 10 or 15 years older than any of the other men in the room. I complete a job application form and wait for my turn to be interviewed.

By the time my name is called, the 30-something year old sales manager tells me he's sorry, but they've already agreed to hire the four individuals for which they have available desks. He says they literally don't have the physical space to hire another person. I'm desperate, and certainly not willing to take NO for an answer.

He tells me that they're paying a ten percent commission on all funds received. I offer to use my own phone and work out of my personal home if they'll pay me the same ten percent commission for any funds that I bring in. I ask if he'll give me some of their sales material and lead sheets. He's willing to humor me and I leave with some background material, marketing brochures and a couple of lead sheets.

I immediately return home, spread the sheets on the bed and ask Ashley to please keep the kids quiet. I go right to work. I spread the phone lead sheets out on the bed, get on the phone and start calling physician's offices.

Do you have any idea how hard it is to actually get a doctor on the phone? It takes me two days to schedule the first face-to-face appointment with a doctor.

The following day I deliver the first $10,000 investment check. A few days later I receive a commission check for $1,000. I cash the check and immediately go to the grocery store and load up on enough food to feed the nine mouths at home for a week.

I keep calling out of my bedroom for an additional two weeks and turn in two more checks totaling $20,000. By the time I deliver the third check, the sales manager tells me that they now have a desk open and asks if I'd like to take it. I jump at his offer.

Over the following three or four months, all of the young men that were initially hired have disappeared. Not one of them have succeeded in bringing in money. The sales manager asks me if I know anyone else that I think might be able to help them.

I refer another man that I met when I was first looking for work to One Card. He has a New York accent and appears to be about my age. Ultimately, we two 'old' geezers are the only ones remaining to fund the company. Together, we bring in hundreds of thousands of dollars.

One Card International is soon able to move out their small hole-in-the-wall operation. They lease a good size office building in Culver City, California and formally begin operations. Over the ensuing two years I'm personally responsible for bringing many hundreds of thousands of dollars of investment capital into the company.

While this is going on, our home has again become a magnet for unloved and/or unwanted children. Chuck has a penchant for bringing teen-age boys home with him and our home is always busy. In addition to our nine family members, it seems there are always three to five additional mouths to feed on a daily basis.

I begin shopping at a grocery store in Panorama City that caters to the lowest of low-income Hispanics. I come home many times with sacks full of frozen burritos at ten for a dollar. That's always good as a quick snack for hungry teenagers. Along with additional bags full of whole chickens to bake, shoe-leather chuck steaks to fry, potatoes by the bushel and half gallons of ice cream to scarf down, the ravenous hoard of teenagers' appetites are appeased.

Then, in late summer 1987, my world comes crashing down.

Apparently, a prominent financial services firm in La Jolla has walked off with a bunch of their clients' money. The San Diego District Attorney's office is intent on finding an example they can prosecute for a front-page headline. It looks like I'm the low-hanging fruit.

Two days before the statute of limitations is set to expire, a Grand Jury indictment is issued. The Grand Jury charge is that I've committed 10 counts of securities fraud. I have no money for an attorney. I tell the judge my financial situation and he appoints a young attorney, Daniel Mogin, to provide my defense.

I meet Dan Mogin and get the feeling that he'd rather be fishing. Not really, but he's obviously not relishing the $50 per hour he'll be paid to defend me. Dan asks me to see if I can find any evidence that he might be able to use in my defense. He tells me that he's learned that there are a lot of boxes of business records available and urges me to go through them.

The documents are stored in an upstairs locked room at the main San Diego Post Office. I spend the next four weeks going through 55 legal-size storage boxes containing the entire business and accounting records of CFP, our financial planning firm. The many thousands of pages of records cover over five years of operations. This isn't going to be an easy process.

My weekly routine is brutal. I work Monday through Wednesday to bring in the money my family needs to survive. Then, on Thursday morning, I drive down to San Diego at dawn and spend the day going through documents. Mentally exhausted, I stay the night at my parents' home in North San Diego county, sleeping on a guest bed at least 25 years old.

I spend the entire day Friday going through more boxes of documents before driving back to LA to spend the weekend with my family. This schedule persists for weeks. I'm able to find several dozen documents proving that every financial transaction has been fully documented and no fraud was ever committed.

During this time, Dan Mogin has been talking with the San Diego District Attorney. The DA has decided to modify the governments charges against me. They've agreed to drop all of the charges of securities fraud. They now charge me with a single count of mail fraud. The claim is that I've mailed a Certificate of Limited Partnership to one of my clients without disclosing the loans that CFP has previously made between partnerships.

Dan Mogin tells me that if I can dig up $50,000 that he can use for discovery, he feels sure that I have a 95% chance of beating the DA's charge in court. However, I have no more chance of coming up with that kind of money then I have of flying to the moon.

He suggests perhaps my parents will be willing to put a mortgage on their home. There's even less a chance of that happening.

Finally, just as the trial is about to commence, the District Attorney calls Dan with a settlement offer. If I'll agree to plead guilty to a single charge of mail fraud, they'll recommend 6 months in prison followed by 5 years of supervised probation.

Dan tells me that if I don't accept the offer, he's sure that the District Attorney will insist on a jury trial.

He goes on to say that from his experience, it's almost impossible to know what a jury will do. He says that my chances of winning a jury trial without coming up with money for discovery are probably 50 – 50 at best. Dan says that if I'm found guilty, he's sure the District Attorney will insist I spend 5 years in prison. His recommendation is to accept the DA's offer.

What should I do? I'm almost age 48. Do I risk carving 5 years out of my life in prison? Or, do I bite the bullet and spend 6 months in prison even though I know I'm not guilty?

I decide to go before the judge and plead guilty.

The District Attorney's office never gets the headline that they crave. I'm led away, prepared to spend the next 6 months of my life as a guest of the government.

15 | Prisons

Jesus was a criminal,
or so the people said –
and John spent time in prison
until he lost his head
You've read how Paul and Silas
spent many days in jail
until the earth shook in the night
providing instant bail

The point that these old stories make
along with many modern more
it's not just what the system says
that tells the total score
It isn't what the critics say
or what the judge decrees
or even where your body stays
that keeps you on your knees

It's no shame to be in prison
if it's one run by mankind;
the real shame that ruins lives
are prisons of the mind
Unlock your mind! Unbar the door
that keeps you from your best
and limits your achievements
to no better than the rest

For when your mind knows freedom
and your spirit's soaring free
and you're living your life daily
in peace and harmony
there isn't any record
in dusty history
or shadows playing on the walls
of some long past memory
which can restrict your innate right
to be all that you can be

Larry Brophy

16 | Guest of the Government

I've always been adventurous, but the thought of being a guest of the government in a high security prison has never crossed my mind.

Because my sentence is only 179 days, I'm not scheduled to be assigned to a long-term federal facility. Instead, I'm slotted to spend my next six months in San Diego at the downtown federal metropolitan corrections center, commonly known as the MCC. I learn that the people that are assigned to the facility farcically say that the initials MCC, actually stand for Mexican Country Club.

The building itself is 23 stories tall with a holding capacity of 1,300 inmates. The first couple of floors are primarily administrative, with most of the upper 20 or so floors being plant facilities and inmate housing. Two of the housing floors are dedicated to female inmates.

The central portion of the roof of the building is covered by chain-link fencing, providing a 15-foot high exercise area. For an hour each week, it's the only place to inhale a breath of fresh air. It's a rather forbidding place.

Upon entering, the first thing I'm ordered to do is to get buck-ass naked. I remove all of my civilian clothing and don prison garb. The guard tells me I can have my clothes back when I'm released. I'm photographed, finger-printed and have blood drawn to determine my blood type. I'm assigned to a 7'x10' temporary 2-person holding cell.

I spend the first two weeks holed up with a guy from Northern California who's been convicted of selling 2 kilos of cocaine.

When I learn that he knows how to play backgammon, we ask the guard for a couple of sheets of paper and pencil a backgammon board on one sheet. The other sheet is torn into small pieces for pips and we write numbers on other small pieces to use as dice. Almost every waking hour my first two weeks as a guest of the government is spent playing backgammon.

As the first few days pass by, I make a promise to myself. I'm going to leave this place better physically, mentally and spiritually than when I entered. The last couple of years with Ashley have been hard on me. I've gained 15-20 additional unwanted pounds and my muscle tone has really deteriorated.

I make a commitment to myself that as long as I'm here, I'm going to do something about it.

After two weeks in the intake cell, I'm assigned to another 2-person 7'x10' cell on the 12th floor. The old guy in the cell with me is cantankerous and truly a piece of work. He's unable to speak a single complete sentence without using the word, 'mother-fucker'. Often multiple times. I hear that word spoken more times in a few days than I've heard in decades.

After spending less than a week with him, I tell the guard that I can't take it anymore. I tell the guard, "If you don't get me out of here real quick, I'm going to have to hurt him". He schedules a meeting for me with the 'job coach' the following day. That's not the proper title, but it's his responsibility to assign work jobs for the inmates within the facility.

An interesting thing about a place like this. It's almost a small city. Some inmates are maintenance staff: carpenters, mechanics, painters, etc. Some inmates work in the kitchen, preparing over 1,000 meals, three times a day, or doing KP duty. Others work in the laundry. There's even a barber.

I'm ushered into a small office the next day. The job-coach looks over my work history and asks if I'm willing to serve as the prison librarian. He says that the position has been vacant for a while and thinks I might like it. Heck, I didn't even know there was a library! I immediately accept the job and move into a worker's quad.

The entire seventh floor of the building is dedicated to living space for the inmates performing the duties that keep the prison running. The floor is totally open with no bars or cells. The center of the floor is filled with tables we use for eating meals and playing games like cards, checkers or chess. Each corner of the floor is divided into upper and lower sleeping areas known as quads, each holding 14 double bunkbeds.

I'm assigned to a bottom bunk in Quad B and a guard escorts me down to the 6th floor to meet Ms. Garcia, the manager of inmate services. She's a 50's-something brunette and has obviously seen it all. She looks as hard as nails and will be my new library boss.

My schedule is 8 hours a day, 5 days a week, with an hour for lunch. I'll be paid eighteen cents an hour. There's a designated hour each week for inmates wanting to use the library for each floor. She leads me into the library and shows me how the system works. I'm amazed! There has to be over 5,000 books crammed into a 450 square foot room. Many dozens of shelves are filled with books of any and all genres you can possibly imagine.

There appears to be no rhyme or reason to it. The room is a huge disaster, with many book-covers and pages torn or ripped off. I comment on what a mess it is. She brings out several rolls of book binding tape and tells me I'm free to repair the books if I want.

I ask her if it'd be okay if I organize the library a little bit. She points me to an ancient PC computer and tells me I'm free to use it as well.

I find out why the San Diego MCC was nicknamed, 'Mexican Country Club'. At least half of the inmates are Mexicans who've been caught attempting to cross the border into the U.S., or caught smuggling others into the country. Although they tend to hang out together in a couple of other quads, I develop a warm relationship with them.

After a couple of months, one of them overdoses on a substance a visitor has smuggled in. He comes over to my bunk in tears and I comfort him for over a half hour before the guard finds him and takes him back to his quad. The guard returns and gives me a warning. He tells me that this guy's dangerous and I really ought to be more careful in the future.

A 5.3 magnitude earthquake occurs on October 1st. Even though the quake epicenter is 100 miles away in Whittier, the building rocks and rolls for a minute or more.

For the following two or three months, I look forward to my time in the library each day. I tape up and repair hundreds of books and organize the library into separate sections for each genre.

Rather than the books being all crammed into the backs of the shelves, they're now all organized by author, neatly lined up on the front of the shelves. I find that the computer has a very rudimentary library program and build a database of every book in the library, sortable by title and author.

The inmates that frequent the library are amazed at the transformation taking place. I remember one hard-looking dude in particular. He comes up to me at the desk and said, "Man, I've never seen a library like this. I've been in a lot of joints, and none of them ever had a library this nice". His comment makes me feel good, knowing that I'm able to make a positive difference during the time I'm spending here.

Our evening meal always includes a piece of sheet cake and a piece of fresh fruit, usually an apple or orange. At dinner I ask if anyone wants to trade their fruit for my piece of cake and always have several takers.

I literally wear out the rowing machine on our floor, working up a sweat every day. I find some great personal growth books, read them diligently after work and make time to meditate daily.

I have several visitors during my stay. For a couple of hours on Sundays, friends and family members are allowed to visit for up to an hour. My mother drives down from Vista to spend an hour with me and it's very healing.

Ashley comes down from LA to see me once. It doesn't go particularly well and I go back to my bunk pretty despondent.

Christmas comes and goes. Even though I'm locked up, I see and feel my life changing for the better. Others see the change as well. In early January, Ms. Garcia gives me an overprint book catalogue with hundreds of book titles available for pennies on the dollar.

She tells me she has a book budget of $800 and asks me if I'll go through the catalogue and pick out books that I feel would be best for the inmates. I'm able to order over 250 new books for the library.

The floor above the regular library is the law library, containing over a thousand law books. Ms. Garcia says that many of the law books are badly out of date, resulting in inmates filing appeals based on overturned laws. She asks if I'll be willing to go through the volumes filling the shelves and keep only the current editions.

I fill two laundry carts to the top with old outdated law books, and they're dumped into the big dumpsters behind the building. When I'm through, the shelves contain less than half the number of law books they had before I arrived.

I learn I'm entitled to be released two weeks early for good behavior, but think I might be able to do better. I apply for an early release and Ms. Garcia writes a letter recommending my early release. The guard tells me that she's never done that for any inmate over the preceding ten years.

My early release request is approved and I'm scheduled for release on Tuesday, February 9th, almost a month ahead of schedule.

The last couple of days seem to move glacially. Finally, the moment of freedom arrives. I go down to the first floor and am handed a bag containing the clothes I walked in with along with my wallet. I pull up my old jeans and they almost fall to the floor. My waist is at least 2 or 3 inches smaller than when I arrived. I cinch up my belt, take the $35 that I've saved from my work in the library, and walk to the train station.

I buy a ticket to Los Angeles and call my friend Tyk with the train arrival details.

Now I have to figure out what I'm going to do next.

17 | Florida

Man, what a weird feeling! The simple act of walking to the train station is surreal.

Nobody can tell you what it feels like to come back into society after months being locked up. It's really strange. You feel like you're watching things happen around you while being merely a disinterested observer.

The feeling diminishes over time, but it definitely takes a while before you feel like you're again part of the action. I can only imagine how difficult it must be for those locked away for years.

The Amtrak Pacific Surfliner took a little over three hours to make the trip from San Diego to Los Angeles. I watch the world slide by with a new sense of wonder. For me, the trip is filled with a mixture of relief and anxiety.

Relief at being free again.

Anxiety at not knowing what my future is going to hold.

Tyk is waiting for me when the train arrives. It's a huge relief to see him again. On the drive to his apartment, he brings me up to speed on what's been going on with my family while I've been away. He tells me that Ashley called him the previous week and said that she's moved and doesn't want to see me again.

She told Tyk that she wants to give him the address and key to the storage locker where she has stored my personal belongings. Tyk says he has the key and we'll check it out over the next couple of days.

Interestingly enough, when I hear this it feels like a huge weight is lifted from my shoulders. I know it means that any karmic entanglement between us has been completed.

For the first time in a long time I feel completely free. I call it my 6-years of intensive sensitivity training and never see Ashley again.

The following weekend, Tyk takes me over to the storage unit to retrieve my personal belongings. It's one of the smallest rental storage units available. When I open the door, I can't help but stand there speechless.

Ashley saved my clothes, a few books and my Jucit automatic juicer. She threw away my thousands of photographs covering 25 years of my life along with almost everything else I'd accumulated. I can fit everything I own at this moment neatly into the bed of a pickup truck with room to spare.

I'm basically starting over from scratch.

A couple of weeks later, I receive a phone call out of the blue. Terry Brazzell, one of my original partners in CFP has tracked me down. He heard somewhere that I was no longer a guest of the government and says he wants to discuss a job opportunity with me. He's dropped his last name and now goes by the name of Terry Allen. He tells me he's embarking on a career as a personal development speaker and has founded a company called American Institute of Achievement, or AIA.

Terry says that he's found a financial backer and is planning to launch his business in Naples, Florida. He tells me he wants me to be his national marketing director.

One of the conditions of my plea agreement is that upon release, I agree to serve 5 years of supervised probation. I haven't even met the probation officer I've been assigned to yet. I tell Terry I'll be meeting with my probation officer the following week and will see if I can get permission to accept his offer and move to Naples.

The following week Mr. Silver, the probation officer, and I meet for the first time at his office in Van Nuys. He begins by telling me that I can't leave Los Angeles County without his written permission. After we speak for perhaps 20 minutes, I relay the job opportunity that Terry has offered me. He gives me a quizzical stare.

After what seems like eternity, he says, "I've never done this in the 20 years I've been a probation officer. You're not asking me to go out of the county, but want me to allow you to go all the way across the country. However, I'm going to take a chance on you and give you permission to leave."

He gives me the name and contact information to the probation officer I'll need to check in with in Florida. I leave quickly before he can change his mind.

I call Terry and tell him I can accept his offer. He overnights a plane ticket. When the ticket arrives, it's a one-way ticket to Houston, not Florida. I call him and Terry tells me he has an office in Houston and says we'll all be going to Naples together the following week.

I've slept on the couch at Tyk and Connie's apartment for about a month.

When we arrive in Florida, it's April, spring is in full booom and everything is beautiful. In addition to me, Terry has hired Steve Woerner to be the AIA sales manager. Steve is 10 years my junior, overflowing with energy, with a shiny bald head with a fringe of hair around the sides. He and I lease a home in Naples about 2 blocks from the Gulf coast.

Terry leases a new Cadillac and a $6,000 per month luxurious home on Marco Island. We all settle in and I call my new probation officer. Her office is in the Miami area, all the way across the state from Naples. Although I speak with her monthly on the phone, I never get to meet her.

Steve and I have the job of filling rooms with audiences for Terry to film his personal development training program. We fill hotel conference rooms enough times for Terry to record over a dozen hours of training material. Terry has synthesized the advice of legendary personal trainers like Jim Rohn, putting his personal spin on their words.

In our spare time, of which there is ample, Steve and I enjoy the summer in Naples. We walk two blocks down to the beach every evening and watch the sun sink into the ocean. We spend almost every weekend fishing for greenback mackerel off of the Naples pier and catch a bunch. I learn a great way to 'fry 'em up' and we eat a lot of fresh fish for several months.

However, things aren't all rosy. After I really get to know Terry on a personal level, I learn that he does a great job preaching what people should do to succeed in their lives. Unfortunately, he's unwilling to apply the principles he's teaching in his own life.

I keep asking him to sit down and make a marketing plan with me for when the videotaping is complete, but he seems totally averse to planning. We have confrontations where I tell him that The Universe won't prosper him if he doesn't personally practice what he preaches. I realize that his failing to plan is actually planning to fail.

Terry's plan is to walk into a packed arena, wow the people with a rousing presentation and sell his self-help tapes and videos. When he's through speaking, he wants someone to announce, "Terry Allen has left the room! Don't leave without taking his tapes and video training material home with you". This is certainly not my bag.

I haven't saved much money, but know that the writing is on the wall again. I'm not happy. And I don't want to be part of it. I think I better get back to California.

The best deal I can find is on Amtrak. They have a special promotion going. It allows a traveler to take any four legs that Amtrak goes, anywhere in the country, over a 6 month period for only $200. Heck, I have enough money for that.

The following week in September 1988, Steve and I awake to a glorious Sunday morning. Steve says, "Hey, I just learned that there's a real cool Unity church in Naples. What say we find out where it is and take in a service?". I haven't seen the inside of a church for several years, but say, "Sure. Let's do it!".

We find the church and it is truly cool. It's octagonal in shape with many of the walls filled floor to ceiling with glass. Looking out, all you can see is the green Florida pine forest. We get to the church about 10 minutes before the service begins and Steve finds two seats in the middle of the room towards the front.

We sit behind two women who are chatting amicably. I still remember the subject of the ministers talk. It was, "Let God be God". His advice was not to limit the power of the Source. I appreciate it.

At the end of the service, I stand in line to thank the speaker for delivering such a good talk and tell him how much I enjoyed it. As fate would have it, I stand in line behind one of the women we were seated behind.

I mention to her how much we enjoyed her animated conversation with her friend. Then it's my turn to thank the speaker.

After speaking with him I walk into the bookstore. I'm amazed to find many of the books I've been reading over the past dozen or more years. The woman that we'd been seated behind comes up and taps me on the shoulder. She says, "We didn't have a chance to finish our conversation. Do you have a moment now?"

I learn that her name is Diane Szymanski. She's an outgoing dark-haired brunette a few years younger than me and a full-time Dale Carnegie instructor in Detroit, Michigan. She says she only attended church that day because her flight home has been delayed and she wanted to spend a few more hours with her friend.

We stand in the church courtyard and talk for perhaps 40 minutes. I tell her that I'm planning to leave Naples and go back to Los Angeles.

She pauses for a couple of moments. Then she says, "I'm attending a gala celebration on the Star of Detroit in two weeks. It's to honor Jack Boland, the head minister of The Church of Today, along with Ralph Nichols the Dale Carnegie franchise holder, and Michael Wicket, a personal development speaker. I don't have an escort yet. Would you be willing to stop by Detroit when you leave here and be my escort?"

Although I didn't know it at the time, the decision we made to go to church that day is a pivotal point in my life.

I tell Diane I'll be glad to be her escort and make plans to book the first leg of my Amtrak journey with a stop in Detroit.

Detroit isn't even on my list of the top 100 places I've ever wanted to visit.

Now I'm going there.

18 | MapInfo

It isn't hard for me to leave Florida. Even though I've done a lot of personal healing, the rancor of the past couple of months with Terry Allen has weighed on my spirit. He has a gift to truly help a lot of people, but his own ego is edging the good out of his life. I'm grateful that he offered help when I most needed it, but saddened that our relationship has crumbled.

On Monday, September 28, 1988 I pack a single large suitcase and throw it in the car. I don't even feel like waving goodbye as Steve picks up speed and heads down the Tamiami Trail towards the Amtrak station in Miami.

The Amtrak Silver Meteor leaves late morning, travelling up the east coast to Washington D.C. After a transfer to the Amtrak Capitol Limited, it's on to Chicago. Finally, after yet another transfer to the Amtrak Wolverine, I arrive in Michigan.

I travel for two days and nights and get off the train at the Dearborn, Michigan station. Diane is there to welcome me and drives me to her home. She offers to let me camp out in her daughter's room while I'm a guest. Exhausted, I climb into the single bed and fall asleep, wondering what new adventures await me.

I discover that the colors of the trees in Michigan are magnificent in the fall. I grew up in Southern California and have never seen trees with leaves of such vibrant reds, oranges and yellows. The neighborhood surrounding Diane's home is an absolute cacophony of color. I'm bowled over by the beauty everywhere I look.

The gala celebration I've agreed to attend with Diane comes quickly. The Star of Detroit is packed with both Dale Carnegie and Church of Today members. I sit at the head table with Jack Boland and a dozen others. I can't remember ever experiencing a more enjoyable evening.

After the celebration, Diane, I and about a dozen others go to The Whitney, a Romanesque revival mansion in Detroit turned into a restaurant, for cocktails. I've never met so many friendly, up-lifting people in one place before. What an enjoyable night!

The coming Sunday I attend the Church of Today in Warren, Michigan with Diane. We sit in the first row and there are probably a thousand people in the auditorium. It's packed to the rafters and the atmosphere is electric. Jack Boland gives one of the most uplifting talks I've ever heard.

I have a big decision to make. I have nothing to go back to in California. After the meeting, I tell Diane I'm considering staying in Michigan. She suggests that I attend her next Dale Carnegie class as a guest that coming Tuesday evening and I agree. She introduces me as a guest, and it's a rousing session. There are a lot of laughs all around. After the Carnegie session, she mentions to the 20 or so people in the room that I'm thinking of staying in Michigan.

One of her students is a paraplegic named Jack Lewis. He's wheelchair bound, paralyzed from the waist down. Jack was working under a car sitting on jacks when it fell on him and broke his back a dozen or more years before. Jack pipes up and says that if I want to stay in Michigan, I'm welcome to stay with him at his home in Lapeer. The next day I move my suitcase to Jacks home.

Jack and I attend the Church of Today the following couple of weeks. I'm introduced to Jim Tuman, a single man that works with troubled high school youth. He has a two-bedroom condo in Royal Oak. Although he has an existing roommate, he tells me I'm welcome to make a space to live in his basement if I'm interested.

I rearrange some of the boxes to make an open space and move into his basement.

Now I need transportation and find an ad for an old, rusted out Ford Escort for sale for $600. The owner accepts my offer of $300 down and $75 a month and I'm finally mobile again.

I drive to downtown Detroit to meet my new probation officer. His name is Beau Williams. He's in his mid-50's and has been a federal probation officer for many years. As a probation officer in Detroit, he's truly seen it all.

When he looks at my file, he asks about the $50,000 restitution that I've been ordered to pay. I was able to make 7 or 8 payments of $900 a month, and haven't been able to pay anything on it the past several months.

He reads the court order and notes that the judgement bears no mention of interest. Beau tells me that in the absence or other instructions, court rules are to charge 18% interest on all outstanding debts.

Beau tells me that my attorney should have requested that interest be waived, and suggests my attorney was either sloppy or just didn't care.

I'm flabbergasted.

Even though I've paid thousands of dollars, I now owe more to the government than when I started. I promise to pay $500 a month as soon as I find a job even though I know that amount won't even cover the accruing interest.

We talk for a half hour or more, and I give him copies of two or three of the poems I've written over the past couple of months. He takes them without a single glance.

On my next monthly meeting with him, Beau casually mentions that he went before a judge and that the court has agreed to remove the interest requirement on my restitution agreement. He says that every dollar I've previously paid has been applied to reduce my obligation.

I find it hard to believe he did this for me on his own. My faith in the legal system gets a huge boost and I feel like a millstone has just been lifted from around my neck.

I tell Beau that I'm going to remain in Michigan and request permission to travel back to Los Angeles to pick up the rest of my worldly possessions, using the paid-for train ticket that still has a couple of months remaining before it expires. He gives me permission to go and tells me to check back in with him as soon as I return. I'm definitely on a roll.

In 1989 I continue going to the Church of Today Sunday mornings. That first winter in Michigan, I make ends meet by doing minor home repairs and room remodels for a few of the folks I've met at church.

One of the guys at church hears me sing and introduces me to the Detroit Oakland Chapter of SPEBSQUA, the barbershop harmony society. I join the chorus as a bass and end up singing with them for almost a decade. I spend the final years as the Chapter treasurer.

At the Church of Today, there are two Sunday church services; 9:00 a.m. and 11:00 a.m. I prefer the early service because it doesn't break up my day. Between services they always have a social time, serving hot coffee and deep-fried donut holes.

One Sunday I meet a petite blond woman named Lynne Ditzhazy. We chat amicably for perhaps 10 minutes. She's really cute. I'm attracted to her, but am certainly in no place in my life at this time to have a relationship.

Meanwhile, my old buddy Zachary Taylor calls and says that his company is doing the special effects for The Who band world reunion tour. He says they'll be in Michigan the following month and tells me he can get me a pass to the concert and the best seat in the house. I arrive at The Palace in Auburn Hills a couple of hours before the concert kicks off.

I find a seat on the sound mixing platform about six feet high, right in the middle of the stadium floor. While everyone else is standing on their chairs trying to see the band, I have a seat looking over their heads. The music is fantastic, the lighting is breath-taking and the evening is a great break from the daily grind.

In the Spring, I find a job as a salesman working for Inacomp, a computer retailer. The company soon changes their name to The Lead Group, and focuses on providing corporate connectivity solutions. My Ford Escort dies a final, dishonorable death and I find a used Buick Regal to replace it.

At church, I sign up for a meditation class taught by an associate minister and am surprised to see Lynne, the cute blond I'd met a few months earlier in the same class. After a couple of weeks, I ask if I can take her out for a cup of tea after meditation class. Boy, did the sparks fly between us!

We start going for Sunday walks together at the Kensington Lake Recreation area. On our first date I take her on a 6-mile walk around the lake. To say she isn't prepared for a walk that long is an understatement. It's almost our last date, but fortunately she forgives me.

I tell her the entire sordid story of my past because I don't want to get involved with anyone unless they know everything about me. It's honestly amazing that she goes out with me again, because at that time in my life, I've not been the most stable of characters. I'm happy that she's willing to take a chance on me and our relationship blossoms.

About a year after I join The Lead Group, Dave Gonynor, the young owner, comes up to me and says that he just received an interesting offer. He says that a new desktop mapping software company called MapInfo has contacted him asking if he'd like to become their exclusive dealer for the state of Michigan. He hands me their brochures and asks if I'm interested in becoming the company's mapping specialist.

I read the MapInfo marketing material and it resonates. The software is the first of its genre because it allows a business to display data visually, rather than in a rows and column spreadsheet. For example, it allows a company to see on a map where their customers live, so to better market their products and services. Managing a database visually is new, cutting edge software technology with a lot of potential.

I tell him I'm most interested. I soon become the MapInfo guru in Michigan and demonstrate the software to Ford, GM, Chrysler and many businesses and organizations throughout the state of Michigan. The City of Detroit even becomes one of my customers.

Meanwhile, as Lynne's and my relationship deepens, I realize that I'm still legally married to Ashley. I ask friends in California to locate Ashley and soon have formal divorce papers drawn, signed and filed.

One of the purchasers of MapInfo software is Don Musick. Don is the Michigan sales manager for Sea-Doo personal watercraft. He also bought a database of all registered personal watercraft owners from the State of Michigan and plots them on a map to see where they live. He expects to see them clustered around the many thousands of lakes throughout Michigan, but gets a huge surprise instead.

Don excitedly comes into my office one afternoon and can't wait to show me what he found. He learned that instead of personal watercraft owners living near lakes, they form small clusters all over the map. Most of the clusters are a long way from a lake and each cluster includes many makes and models of watercraft.

He comes to the conclusion that when a personal watercraft is purchased, it's a 'Keeping up with the Jones's" type of situation. When the neighbors see the new toy, they also want one for themselves and purchase their own watercraft.

Don says that if only he could find a list of the names and addresses of the closest dozen or two neighbors to every watercraft purchaser, he'd market to them and help his dealers sell lots more boats. It becomes an obsession with him. Don's a backyard programmer and tries unsuccessfully to write a program to accomplish his goal.

Meanwhile, my personal life is getting really serious. Lynne and I have moved in together in her apartment on 12 Mile Road in Southfield. In mid-1991 we decide to buy a place together.

We find a 2-bedroom condominium in West Bloomfield, scrape together enough money for the down payment and close escrow. The place is horribly outdated, with all of the walls and even some of the ceilings covered with wallpaper. However, we have plans to turn it into our dream condo.

The evening after we close escrow, we walk into our new place and I start ripping out the old carpet. Lynne is aghast! She thought we'd spend the first night celebrating with a bottle of wine, but instead, I go right to work. Luckily, she forgives me for that, too.

After a couple of months, I cut a big hole in the middle of the dining room floor. I head off the floor joists and install a spiral staircase joining the walkout basement and living area. It's to be only the first of many major remodels we do in our life together.

On advice of our CPA, we decide to wait until after the first of the year to get married. On January 24, 1992 we meet at the Church of Today. Jack Lewis and

131

Lynne's sister Joyce are our witnesses. The associate minister that performs the ceremony tells us that when she marries couples, they stay married. After my previous marital experiences, I sure hope she's right.

During my time at The Lead Group I attend many training sessions provided by vendors. One of the men I meet is a Black man running the training department at the local IBM office named Murray Davis. He's well educated and very articulate.

After one of the training sessions, we discuss the insights that Don Musick discovered using the MapInfo software. Murray gets really stoked. I introduce him to Don and we meet several times.

We sketch out a possible solution combining maps with a national address file and a national household demographic database. Don, Murray and I talk about starting a software company to develop the capability to locate the neighbors of each Sea-Doo purchaser. We brainstorm all the different types of businesses that can benefit from the technology.

Man, it seems like just about any kind of retail or service benefit can benefit – especially the small businesses that are always looking for more local customers.

Don loves the idea, but isn't interested in creating a new company. He has a real good gig going and doesn't want to rock his financial boat. Murray and I aren't similarly constrained and continue meeting and planning.

After several more months of discussion and a ton of personal research, we decide to form a company. Our goal is to develop and market a software product that can create highly targeted marketing lists for any company, using their own customer database.

The new company is formed, and we call it GeoDemX, combining both 'geographics' and 'demographics'.

Murray and I start putting together a business plan. We're confident we can attract an investor and I put in my two-week notice.

Now age 52, another new adventure has begun.

19 | GeoDemX

I've learned that when multiple roadblocks appear in front of you, you're better off rethinking your course. Conversely, when difficulties quickly vanish, you're probably doing something right and need to re-double your efforts. Fortunately, as we begin the new adventure of GeoDemX, things flow smoothly and our confidence grows.

Our business goal is to create a product which will help small businesses increase their profitability. The best way to do that is to help companies provide their products and services to more people. Just about everyone that's been around for any length of time knows that the most important asset of any business are their customers.

Without enough customers, a business can't cover overhead and pay salaries, much less prosper. To solve this problem, many companies spend a big piece of their revenue on a marketing budget trying to find more customers, often with mixed results.

A businessman might know that a whole lot of people living in his community need his product or service, but how does he get them in the door?

This is the part that we want to address. Most small to mid-size businesses struggle in this area. Virtually every business around is interested in obtaining additional new customers for fewer marketing dollars.

This becomes our primary focus, and the entire purpose of our new software company: To create a marketing tool that will help a business identify their most likely future customers.

We call our new software product "GeoWizard".

We know how we want our marketing tool to work and flesh out the design for our new software product. Our challenge is to contract for and manage the many types of data required. Once we locate the data providers, we must convince them to grant us a master re-seller license to include their data into our software.

Our task is to seamlessly pull all of this data together into one simple-to-use product. It's really quite an audacious challenge.

GeoWizard combines street level maps of every street in the country, a database containing the name, address and phone number of every person, and a third database of demographic and psychographic information on every household in America. As personal information is constantly changing, updates must be made available on a regular basis.

And, the software has to run on a normal personal computer. The sheer size of the databases involved is absolutely staggering.

The principle behind GeoWizard is to use your own best customers to find other people just like them. By modeling their age, income, home ownership, family status, hobbies, and more, GeoWizard generates a marketing list of similar people in your market area.

The software runs on your own personal computer, contains all of the data required, and can be run when and as frequently as desired.

The concept is revolutionary. No other product has ever been created that provides marketing lists of this fine granularity to date. The software will use MapInfo to provide the mapping aspect required. It also gives us the ability to manage the databases visually.

Even though we've not approached any of the major players in the data world, I'm confident we can pull it off. I convert the downstairs walkout basement of our condo into an office and add another phone line. A two-foot wide piece of oak sitting on top of a couple of two-drawer filing cabinets becomes my desk. We find a used desk and a buy a couple of office chairs and book shelves and we're ready to go to work.

The year is 1993. GeoDemX has been formed, and we're now in business.

I'm installed as the company president. Murray and I build a list of people to speak with and begin making phone calls.

While planning our new adventure, I continue selling MapInfo software and supplemental data to take care our personal cash flow needs. We're introduced to a dentist and a professional investor who both love our concept and provide the seed capital to begin operations.

We fly to Little Rock and drive over to Conway, Arkansas to meet with the president of Axciom Corporation. Acxiom is a database marketing company and has compiled a database containing the name, address and phone number of every household in America.

The president of Acxiom tells us if we're able to pull GeoWizard off, he thinks it'll revolutionize marketing for small businesses. We sign master re-seller agreements with Axciom for their national address/phone database.

We drive over to Schaumberg, Illinois to meet with the folks from Experian. Most people think of them as only a credit reporting company, but they're much more. Experian is a major data aggregator and stores the household level demographic and psychographic data on every person and household in America. We sign master re-seller agreements with them as well. Both companies like our marketing idea and give us added support and encouragement.

We lease office space on the 9th floor of a 17-story office building in Southfield, Michigan and build out the space to meet our needs. We're fortunate to hire two key employees.

Dr. Marc Konvisser, a math professor at Wayne State University is a brilliant man. He becomes our chief programmer. Marc learns MapBasic, the programming language for MapInfo, and quickly writes thousands of lines of code.

Ken Sivaraman, one of the geekiest of geeks, becomes our systems engineer and puts together the hardware required to develop GeoWizard. I've never seen Ken in a pair of pants. He always wears a pair of shorts, even in Michigan's coldest, sub-freezing, bone-chilling days of January and February.

The problem most difficult to solve, and the thing that almost sinks our ship, is the incredible size of the database files we must manage. The size of a single database file often exceeds several gigabytes. Somehow, between Ken and Marc, they find and implement the cutting-edge technology that allows GeoWizard to work.

From a technological perspective, what we're trying to do is ahead of its time. We're like the froth on the edge of the information wave. It takes a bank of the biggest, baddest, fastest PC computers on the market at this time to crunch the vast quantities of data. We actually buy chains of 9GB SCSI hard drives for over $10,000 a pair.

To put that into perspective, your cellphone today has many times that much storage capacity.

As we progress, I become Marc's software tester. Marc will roll out a new feature and tell me, "Give it a whirl and see if you can break it". I'm often able to break the software within a few minutes, when he'll say, "Okay, give it back to me and let me fix it".

Marc's favorite saying is, "My knowledge may only be an inch wide, but it's a mile deep". We're truly fortunate to have him associated with the company.

Ken is the prototypical geek. He's constantly living in the midst of that foam at the leading edge of a wave. He's young, but a brilliant computer engineer. He can put just about any type of equipment together and make it work. He works seamlessly with Marc and GeoWizard is born. We hire an artist to create a product logo and print thousands of four-color brochures.

We attend several national marketing and software conventions and rent booths displaying

GeoWizard's capability. We have excellent feedback from the early purchasers of GeoWizard.

One of our most vocal supporters is a national deck company headquartered in Virginia. They find that their most receptive prospects are homeowners with household incomes over $50,000, living within a block of one of their new deck customers.

Every time they install a new deck, they use GeoWizard to locate their ideal customers and mail a postcard showcasing the newly completed deck to the 20 closest households matching their criteria. It works wonderfully, and their business grows. Their glowing testimonials help sell many copies of GeoWizard.

Although software sales are taking place, as a new company we have a burn rate that exceeds our revenue. We soon discover a major hurdle that we find difficult to overcome. Although the principle behind GeoWizard is sound, our technology is revolutionary and difficult for many small business owners to comprehend.

Or maybe, we just didn't develop a simple enough way to present it. In any case, we're definitely pioneers in the target-marketing world.

GeoWizard is the subject of a great feature article written up in a national mapping publication that helps clarify the process for many. The cover article generates additional inquiries and we're able to make a few more sales.

Now that the product is complete and being positively received, we need to boost sales. We hire a couple of additional salespeople, but that seems to do little to decrease our negative cash flow.

After a few months, the need for additional capital to expand our business is becoming desperate. It gets to the point where we don't know if we're going to be able to make next month's office lease payment.

I fly to San Francisco with Lynne to present GeoWizard to a venture capital group. Unfortunately, the stress I'm under kicks off a massive gout attack. I spend the day sequestered in our hotel room, unable to walk.

The day of the presentation, I can't get my dress shoes on both feet. So, I wear a three-piece suit with a dress shoe on my right foot and a loosely laced tennis shoe on my left foot.

I go to the building address on Market Street and enter a conference room on the 22nd floor. The wall at the end of the room is floor to ceiling glass overlooking the city. At the large table sit 4 or 5 angel investors and venture capitalists. I join a dozen other young entrepreneurs in the conference room pitching their ideas.

I'm the sixth or seventh to make a presentation and in a lot of pain. Needless to say, I'm not anywhere near my best and fly back home empty-handed.

Just as the hands of the clock are poised at one minute before midnight, we receive a call from American List Corporation, a public company based in New York. Their primary product is selling compiled lists of every school child in America. They operate as American Student List Company. The company is more than 30 years old and their stock is traded on the American Stock Exchange.

They want to schedule a visit to our offices and discuss the possibility of buying GeoDemX.

We greet American List's President, COO and Executive Assistant and go through a complete demonstration of GeoWizard and its capabilities. We answer many questions and our guests review our entire operation.

They love GeoWizard and tell us they'd like Murray and me to visit their offices on Long Island the following week. They arrange a limo to pick us up at Kennedy Airport and we're impressed with their offices.

Once we've been given a tour of their operation, we all enter a conference room. We're surprised that they've already drawn up all of the legal documents, with only a few blank spaces to be filled by hand. The offer is good for us.

They'll infuse a six-figure amount into GeoDemX immediately, pay Murray and me all the back salary we're owed, and we reserve the right to re-acquire the company if things don't work out. We discuss their offer, fill in the blanks, and they agree to purchase GeoDemX.

The purchase agreement is drawn and signed, and they infuse a significant amount of cash into the company. We were actually less than 30 days from declaring bankruptcy and now the world is bright again.

Sales improve, and our cash flow bleed rate slows, but revenue never quite catches up with expenses.

About a year later the COO of American List calls and says that they're making an announcement the following day. He says that American List has been purchased by Snyder Communications, a major direct marketing company, and wants us to know ahead of time.

Snyder Communications is traded on the New York Stock Exchange, and GeoDemX will now be a subsidiary of a much larger company. The president of the company is Daniel Snyder, the owner of the Washington Redskins football team.

Shortly thereafter, Murray Davis' life begins falling apart. His wife meets someone who will pay attention to her and files for divorce after more than 20 years of marriage. Murray suspects that one of his three children is not his biological child, runs DNA tests, and his suspicion proves true.

He becomes consumed with his personal problems and our relationship hits the rocks. He is detached, almost belligerent, and it becomes increasingly difficult to work with him.

The following months are tense. I start getting gout attacks every couple of months. The last year we work together, I have six gout attacks, sometimes affecting both feet.

The pain is almost unbearable as I attempt to navigate all day on a pair of crutches. It becomes obvious to everyone we can't continue to work like this.

The final nail in the coffin of GeoDemX is driven in early 1996. We receive another phone call from the COO of American List. He tells us that Snyder Communications is in discussions to be purchased by a Dutch company in a multi-billion dollar deal and they don't want the GeoDemX division.

Under the terms of our sales agreement with American List, they return our stock and tell us we are again on our own.

Murray quickly leaves and the other employees are all let go. I'm still paying rent on an office full of desks, computers and office equipment, but now there's nothing to do.

I close the GeoDemX bank account. Fortunately, I've made many contacts in the direct marketing list business while running GeoDemX. Now's the time to leverage those relationships.

20 | FTD

It's amazing how something that appears on the surface to be so devastating can feel so liberating. Now that American List has cut GeoDemX free, the daily dark cloud of Murray Davis' foul moods has lifted. I no longer feel any personal pressure to perform to anyone else's expectations but my own. The office now seems huge and the data processing room no longer resonates with the constant hum of busy computers.

Right after the phone call from the American List COO, Lynne and I decide to form a new company and name it Focus Marketing Group, Inc. Lynne is volunteered to become the office manager and takes care of all the administrative aspects of running our business.

It's both amazing and rewarding how well we work together. This is sure not Lynne's favorite thing to do, but she's a real trooper.

Fortunately, I receive a phone call from one of the contacts I made almost a year ago. I'd approached the FTD corporate office in Downers Grove, IL about integrating a private label delivery mapping capability with their ordering system for all of their independent U.S. florists. The man I originally met with is no longer with FTD, but my original proposal is apparently still floating around.

The woman now in charge of the FTD software division, Watha Muckler, says they're finally ready to talk about it. I agree to meet her in Downers Grove the following week. Now I have a problem. I'm a one-man show. Who I can find to write and support the program?

I know a red-headed Irishman about my age, John Healy, who owns Healy Corporate Solutions, a small software company just down the street. He writes and supports the bidding software that all of the Class A contractors for the State of Michigan use for bidding bridge and road construction jobs. A while ago John bought MapInfo and MapBasic, the mapping programming language from me.

I decide to tell him about the FTD opportunity and see if he has any interest.

When we meet, John's excited about the potential and agrees to join me in the four-to-five-hour drive to Downers Grove the following week. We agree to split any revenue that might result from the meeting. We have great rapport and get to know each other on the long drive.

We arrive at the FTD corporate offices and are ushered up to the third floor where the FTD Advantage team is located. Watha Muckler is waiting for us and we begin brainstorming what kind of capability they're looking for. After an hour, it's apparent to all of us that we can produce a product that will significantly enhance the FTD Advantage order/accounting system.

Watha Muckler is definitely memorable. She's in her mid-40's, a chain smoker, with a lit cigarette constantly in her hand or burning in an ashtray. Watha was raised in Kentucky and speaks with a strong southern accent.

She has complete authority over the FTD software system and John, Watha and I get along

145

famously. Watha signs a contract with Focus Marketing Group to be the exclusive provider for the FTD Advantage accounting system mapping function.

Over the ensuing two months, John and I fly or drive back and forth between Detroit and the Chicago area several times. John's able to attach hooks into the FTD accounting system and seamlessly pull the order details into the mapping delivery system.

Although the software isn't quite ready to roll out, Watha invites John and me to the FTD regional florists' convention in Nashville, TN after the Easter holiday. We speak with many florists from the U.S. Southeast region and all of us are encouraged to see the excitement for this new capability.

However, Watha's highest priority is to demonstrate the software at their annual national FTD convention, to be held in October, 1996 at the El Conquistador Golf resort in Oro Valley, Arizona. She asks both John and me to attend. FTD treats us as they would any of their employees and offers to pay all of our travel and lodging expenses.

Both John and I bring our spouses along for the adventure and they gladly join us.

At the convention, we have a great time and demonstrate the software many times over 3 days. It's a lot of fun and the florists give us helpful feedback on the new FTD mapping capability. The most important part is that FTD is able to reel in several dozen orders for the new system. Everyone is happy.

I'm the mapping guy and work with each florist around the country to determine their precise local delivery area. I create a custom 3' by 4' full color wall map for each florist, contracting with a local blueprint company to provide the prints. I'm able to produce each map in extremely fine detail and upload the actual plotter image to the blueprint company online. It's a seamless process and a nice source of revenue for us.

The capability that we've brought to the FTD Advantage accounting system results in many more orders, and the folks at FTD are stoked to be ahead of all of their software competitors.

While we're designing and implementing the FTD software, I'm simultaneously learning the intricacies of the marketing list business. While promoting GeoWizard, I met many marketing professionals.

I now concentrate on developing professional business relationships with all sorts of data aggregators and compilers. I purchase the SRDS catalogue containing the description of every type of list available and continue selling direct marketing lists to bring in much needed revenue.

A year quickly passes, and in late summer 1997, FTD again invites John and me to participate in the Annual FTD National Convention in October. This time it's in Hawaii. FTD buys us airline tickets and pays for a week lodging at the Hilton Hawaiian Village hotel in Waikiki Beach. Obviously, it's an opportunity for another holiday.

John Healy is accompanied by his wife, Char, and Lynne joins me along with her son John, who agrees to chaperone us on our adventure. We all have a great time and FTD proudly displays their delivery mapping system.

Another benefit comes out of our time in Hawaii. In early 1998 we receive a call from Bachman's, the largest privately held florist in the Midwest. They watched us demonstrate the FTD mapping delivery system in Hawaii, and want to know if we can develop the same system for them. They're using a much more robust order/accounting system and have 23 different floral shops in the greater Minneapolis and St. Paul area.

We agree to fly out and meet with them.

It's the most professional floral operation we've ever seen. In addition to the 23 different shops, they have a central delivery location and have broken down their market area into 80 different delivery zones. John figures out how to retrieve the necessary data from their proprietary system and I figure out how to create the highly specific zones they require. We sign a high 5-figure contract, develop and install the software by mid-1998.

However, both Lynne and I are getting tired of the long hours I'm working. The long winters in Michigan, often lasting 5 months or more, are also getting us down. We decide it's time to look for somewhere else to call home.

We sit down and draw up a list of everything that we want in a home. Our first criteria is that it has to have a view. We love the forest, so it has to be somewhere in or near the mountains. Because we need to travel, being within 2 hours of a major airport is also important.

However, it can't be in the sticks. The town needs to have a population of at least 10,000 to provide a mix of retail businesses.

Our home also needs enough space for a dedicated office. Although I don't know what kind of work I'll be doing, it has to have a space big enough to be used as an office.

Oh, two more things.

Lynne is guardian and caretaker for her son John, who's handicapped from a traumatic brain injury suffered in an auto accident 13 years ago when he was 18 years old. John will be coming with us, so our home needs to have enough space to accommodate his needs.

The other requirement is no mosquitos. It also has to be located in a mosquito free area because of my allergy to mosquito bites. We look at a map and I draw 100-mile radii around several major airport hubs.

As I have no interest in going back to California, the areas that provide all of the criteria we're looking for appear to be located in Colorado, New Mexico or Arizona. It looks like we'll be moving west. We begin looking for prospective towns we might want to call home and buy 6-month subscriptions to the local newspapers of several communities meeting our criteria.

That way we'll get a flavor of the type of residents in each town and what kind of weather we can expect.

The die has been cast. We're going to beat it out of Michigan.

21 | The Move

Now that Lynne and I've made the decision to leave Michigan, the number one question on our mind is, "Where do we want to live?". After reading the local Durango, Colorado newspaper for a couple of months, we decide that the winters are too cold. Plus, there's more snow than we want to deal with.

Reading the Show Low, Arizona local paper editorial and opinion sections doesn't give us a feeling that it has the friendly community spirit that we're looking for.

Sedona, Arizona looks very enticing, but we don't know if we can afford a home there. Reading the Payson Roundup newspaper makes us think that Payson, Arizona could be a strong contender.

It's mid-summer in Michigan, and there's only one way to find out. We've got to check things out in person. We rent a 25-foot motorhome for a week online and fly into Phoenix to pick up our new wheels. We want to check out Sedona first and hit the road.

Sedona is a beautiful area and the red rock formations are breath taking. We spend two days there and fall in love with the area. However, the price we'll have pay for a home providing all of the amenities we require is way over our budget.

We drive down I-17 to the greater Tucson area and love the high desert terrain, but don't know if we can handle the summer heat.

We end our week on the road with a couple of days in Payson. This small community, home to just over 10,000 residents, is in the middle of the largest Ponderosa Pine forest in the world at an elevation of 5,000 feet. Payson's in the exact middle of the state, less than two hours north of the Phoenix airport.

The price for the kind of home that has everything we're looking for is at least a hundred thousand dollars under similar homes in Sedona. The town is large enough to have a reasonable collection of retail businesses and amenities. We decide that we'll take the plunge and look for a new home in Payson.

As soon as we get back to Michigan, we list our condo in West Bloomfield with a local realtor. In less than 14 days we receive a purchase offer for 20% more than any of the other 75 condominiums in our development has ever sold for.

The remodel that we've done to improve this place will sure provide a nice nest egg. We accept the offer on the condition that we have at least 45 days to find a new place to land and move our stuff out.

I call the largest ERA real estate office in Payson and ask to speak to an agent with a minimum of 5 years of real estate experience. I'm connected to Joy Richards and describe what we're looking for. I tell her that we'll be in Payson the following week and will have 4 days to find and buy a home, but not just any home.

If it doesn't have a gorgeous view, please don't waste both of our time showing it to us.

I ask for her best lender referral, remit our financial information and get pre-approved for a loan. How we get approved for a quarter-million dollar loan without having a job or a source of income has to be one of the most amazing miracles of the year.

Joy is ready for us when we arrive at her office. She has a list of a half-dozen homes that she thinks might meet our needs. The initial homes she shows us all have one or more flaws and we're feeling a little despondent. However, she saves the best one for last.

When she opens the front door, all we can do is stand there and say, "Wow!". We're looking through a wall of glass over a forest of trees all the way to the Mogollon Rim some 20 miles away. The home is amazing.

It turns out that this home was built by the owner of Blandford Homes, a large luxury home builder in the Phoenix area, for his father. It's brand new, unlived in, and actually not on the market at the moment. But, Joy thinks it might be available.

She knows that the senior Blandford had listed the home for a short time before removing the listing when he decided to move into the home himself. Although he's stacked a bunch of boxes in the garage, he hasn't fully moved in yet. Joy said he just had a minor stroke and will require ongoing medical treatment that isn't available at the local Payson hospital. She thinks he won't want to make the drive from Payson to Phoenix 5-days a week for treatment.

We ask her to submit a full-price offer.

She calls him the next day with our offer and he agrees to sell the home to us. When she gives us the good news, we're ecstatic and drive back out to the property in the afternoon. A double rainbow appears over the house as we pull up. As it turns out, we've found our new home in only two days! The Universe is definitely smiling upon us.

We fly back to Michigan and start packing.

The logistics of the move are daunting. Not only do we have to move all of our household furniture and personal effects, but we also have to close down the office and move a significant amount of business furniture and equipment. As our son John will be coming to Arizona with us, we'll have to pack up all of his personal belongings and move him as well.

We make a list of all of the things in our office that we won't be needing in our new home office and print up flyers for a big 'office moving-out sale' the following Friday. It's amazing how much stuff you can accumulate in a short time. I drop the flyers off at every office on each of the 17 floors of our building.

We're able to sell hundreds of dollars' worth of stuff we can live without. As it is, we'll still be hauling two executive desks, tables, office chairs, shelving, 3 or 4 desktop computers, a laser printer, and enough office supplies to last several years.

We pick Sunday to move out of the office. I know that our lease won't be up for another year and decide to empty the space while the property manager isn't in the building. I write a letter for the property manager explaining the circumstances and leave it under their door.

I rent the biggest Ryder truck available and bring along three or four of the strongest young men that our family knows. We begin loading the office first. My God, what a lot of stuff! We pack the desks first, and fill all the desk drawers. The office alone takes up over half of the space in the truck, packed tightly all the way to the roof.

Fortunately, John's personal effects don't take up a lot of space, and we're able to move him out in a couple of hours. Then it's on to our condo. By this time, Lynne's other three children and their friends are all on hand to help us with the final loading.

The entire truck is literally packed to the roof. It takes three people to hold everything in place while we close the truck door. I'll be driving the truck, towing the Ford station wagon we bought from Lynne's dad. It's also pressed into service. The car is completely filled with all of our electronics and office equipment. Two mattresses are tied onto the roof and we look like a modern version of the Beverly Hillbillys.

John will ride in the truck with me and Lynne will follow us in her black Lincoln Mark 8. Not a cubic inch of space is left unfilled. We hug and kiss everybody goodbye and pull away.

The drive is 2,000 miles and it takes us four long days to get to Payson. On the way through Colorado, we have to pass through the foothills of the Rockies. As fate would have it, we go through the mountains about nine o'clock at night in the rain. At times the rain comes down so hard that the windshield wipers have a hard time keeping up.

I have the gas pedal of the truck pressed all the way to the floor. I haven't been able to get out of first gear for a half hour and have a top speed of 15 miles per hour. Thank God Lynne is behind us with her emergency lights flashing. After a couple of hairy hours, we finally make it all the way to the top of the grade.

It's September, 1998 and we finally arrive in Payson to begin our new adventure. I'm able to hire a couple of young movers, we get the truck and car unloaded, and the big pieces of furniture are put in place. Our new home is absolutely perfect. I have a large walk-out basement for an office with a wall of windows overlooking a sea of trees. John has his own bedroom and private bath adjoining the office.

We get the office organized and I'm ready to start business. I'm now almost age 58 and still owe thousands of dollars to the government. We're in a brand-new town and I don't have a job.

I'm sure that we'll find a way to make things work. I just have to find a way to bring in some money.

Again....

The first thing you notice about Payson is the fresh air. It's reported that the town has the purest, least polluted air west of the Mississippi. Payson is located at the foot of the Mogollon (pronounced "Mug'-ee-on") Rim, below the lip of the 7,000' elevation Colorado Plateau, 20 miles to the east.

Our new home is part of a residential development called 'Alpine Heights'. We sit atop a ridge with a wide, unobstructed view of the forest below, all the way to the Rim. We're in town, but the forest is literally outside our back door. Our home overlooks Chaparral Pines Golf Resort, a collection of million dollar-homes surrounding a championship level golf course.

We decide that we need a dog and go to the local animal shelter. We fall in love with a 6-month old, overgrown 60-pound puppy. We learn he's half yellow lab and a quarter each golden retriever and white German shepherd. He's really friendly. We can't understand why he's in an animal shelter. The woman at the shelter says it's because it was reported he's destructive.

I say, "Destructive? How so?" She says that his original owner was a Japanese lady who complained that he pulls her clothes off of the clothes line! He'd been given the name Archimedes.

We adopt him and change his name to Buddy.

When we get home, I put him on a long lead just outside the sliding glass door of my walk-out basement office. I hear Buddy whimpering, look out the window and see a big boar javelina stalking him. He's within 20 feet of Buddy! I jump up from the desk and rush out, shouting and waving my arms.

The javelina takes off, but comes back about 10 minutes later with a dozen of his pals. Again, I jump up, this time throwing rocks at his crew and bring Buddy inside. The fence we have to put up to protect our 'free' dog costs us $2,000.

Fortunately, FTD is still providing us with some income from the sale of our mapping delivery system. And because I'm able to create the wall maps here in Payson and send the plotter files to the blueprint company in Michigan online, the move hasn't affected that part of our income stream. However, it's not nearly enough to pay our bills. I've learned that I can make a decent income in the list business.

I just need to find a way to reach people all over the country. It's now late in 1998 and it looks like I better become familiar with the internet.

It's amazing how things often happen sychronistically. Just as I'm trying to figure out how I'm going to learn enough about the internet to be able to generate leads for Focus Marketing Group, I get a big marketing packet in the mail. It's from the Abraham Group, announcing an upcoming seminar taking place in a hotel near the airport in Los Angeles three months from now.

It's no ordinary seminar. The name of the seminar is, "How to Make a Million Dollars in Internet Marketing". It's a three-day event. And, the price tag is steep. A ticket to the event is $5,000.

I've heard about the guy promoting the event. Jay Abraham is one of the highest paid marketing consultants in the country. I'd love to attend, but we really don't have the money. I call the phone number listed for more information and explain my situation. The gent I speak with tells me that they've had a lot of similar calls and have created a way for me to attend.

If I can send them a check for $2,000 now, they'll reserve a spot and I can pay the balance over the next couple of months. It's a tough nut for us to crack. We just moved into our new home and have a lot of expenses, but I think it's something I really need to do.

I write the check and put the envelope in the mail. I'm attending the seminar in Los Angeles in April.

The day before the seminar I drive to L.A. and get a hotel room for the next few days. I'm one of about 140 seminar attendees and the room is completely sold out. The commercial opportunities that the internet promises are rapidly becoming apparent.

Jay Abraham opens the event with an explanation of how it all came about.

Jay said that as a strategic business consultant, he didn't know enough about internet marketing in today's business environment. So, he contacted the most knowledgeable and successful internet marketers in the country and arranged for them to share everything they know at this seminar. He offers them the opportunity to promote their consulting services to a room full of good prospects.

The big difference is that all 140 of us are each paying him $5,000 to ride along. What a brilliant, sneaky thing to do. He'll learn the same things I will and make a half million dollars at the same time! No wonder he's so successful.

The lineup of speakers is literally a who's-who of internet marketing. The event runs from 9:00 a.m. until 6:00 p.m. each day for three days. Literally every aspect of internet marketing is covered and I discover some of the speakers are currently making a 6-figure monthly income from the internet.

I take page after page of notes and can't wait to get back home to begin to put my new-found knowledge to work.

I quickly learn that it isn't as easy to do as it is to say. The importance of your web address, called the URL, is the first obstacle to overcome. All the simple, short, easy-to-remember names have already been taken. After a lot of time researching URL's on GoDaddy.com, I settle on "FindMoreBuyers.com". I think that aptly describes our business.

The next obstacle is creating a website. I look at all of the top-ranked direct marketing list websites for ideas and tips and learn how the web pages are created. The programing language used to create a webpage is called "HTML", or hyper-text markup language.

I soon learn how to use HTML to create beautiful web pages. However, that's just the beginning. Having a beautiful page doesn't mean a thing if nobody sees it. So, the next thing is to learn how to drive eyeballs to the website.

Each page of the website must be optimized for key words and phrases so the search engines will position your website near the top of the listings for those key words. I write a couple of dozen articles on sales leads, direct mailing, direct marketing, list generation, etc. and post the articles on many article websites for others to use. Each article is rich in key words and contains links to our company name and URL.

Many of my articles are picked up and posted on other websites and FindMoreBuyers.com quickly rises in the search engine listings. I'm able to get a toll-free number, 1-800-LIST, and the phone starts ringing. And ringing.

Lynne and I form a new business entity and call it FindMoreBuyers.com, Inc. I soon find myself so busy answering the phone that it sometimes becomes a real fire drill. After a few months, I'm again working 12 hours a day. The money is good, but I don't have time to turn around and spit.

About this time Tyk calls me from L.A. He tells me that his life has turned upside down. He's at the end of his rope and doesn't know what to do. I ask him if he's interested in moving to Payson and helping me out.

Tyk tells me he has financial obligations and isn't able to get out of town, so I send him some money. He agrees to come work for us and drives to Payson. We have an unused guest room, so I get to return the favor that Tyk gave me when I ceased being a guest of the government. It's a win-win situation.

Tyk has a place to stay while he gets his life back together and I get some much-needed help. After a few months Tyk's able to get his own apartment and life levels off for all of us.

That is, until September 11, 2001. Tyk calls just before 7:00 a.m. and says, "Turn on the TV immediately! I'm on my way over". We turn on the TV and see smoke billowing out of the North Tower of the World Trade Center. Tyk runs in the front door and together we watch in dismay as another plane crashes into the South Tower. We sit for a while in shock, trying to digest what's happening. An hour later the first Twin Tower collapses, followed shortly thereafter by the collapse of the second Twin Tower.

We're numb at the reports of a third and fourth plane hijacking. We think that this might be the start of a major war and our concern is off the chart.

Needless to say, our business phone doesn't ring today. Or the next. Business is the last thing on our minds, and probably will for the next couple of weeks. It takes almost a month before our business regains any semblance of normality.

Once the phone starts ringing again, I realize that we need to add another person to the payroll. Lynne's been taking care of all of our administrative duties, and is being stretched pretty thin. She's still responsible for our son John, and between taking care of John, our home and the business, there's more pressure on her than either of us is comfortable with.

We place an ad in the local paper for an administrative assistant, and interview the three most promising candidates. Toby Schollmeyer, a 30's something ball of energy is our pick and Lynne is finally able to step back from her office duties. Toby fits in well with the rest of us and in a short time, we're all busy.

I continue to market and promote our website presence and the phone bill for our toll-free number quickly exceeds $1,000 per month.

I've made some great connections in the list business and have access to literally thousands of list resources. I develop a particularly close relationship with Manas Mohanty, the owner of American Data Management in Cape Coral, Florida. Manas is from India and a real data professional. Our long-distance friendship soon flourishes.

FindMoreBuyers.com's relationship with ADM now gives us the inhouse capability of running highly specialized list queries. My many years of varied business experience make it easy to help my clients. Now, the thing that's bugging me most is the number of hours I have to sit in front of this computer each week to maintain our search engine rankings.

Our personal life is undergoing some changes now as well. John's been living with us for the past 5 or 6 years and really wants his own place. We find a vacant lot about a mile from our home with lots of trees, backing up to a green belt.

Lynne and I sell some of John's mutual funds, buy the lot and visit a local manufactured home dealer. We find and buy a cute 3-bedroom 1,200 square foot home and have it moved onto the lot. John moves in and we both gain some much-needed privacy and personal space.

I've not created any of the wall maps for florists for the past couple of months and call Watha at FTD. She says that they've acquired a new mapping delivery program to integrate with the FTD Advantage System and thanks me for the time we worked with them. It's bittersweet, but I understand. We've not updated the software for a couple of years.

I'm grateful for the income they've provided. It supported us through some pretty lean times.

In an effort to find a way to relieve the monotony of the daily grind, we acquire a 25' travel trailer and spend many weekends in the beautiful forests surrounding Payson.

We even take an RV trip back to Michigan to spend a couple of weeks with the family. On the way home, we're on the freeway in a thunderstorm just outside of St. Louis, when I glance up and see a sea of red brake lights in front of us. We're in the left lane and there's no place to go.

I hit the brakes, the wheels lock up, and we don't even slow down. Without thinking, I swerve to the left and slide just inches alongside the center divider past a half dozen cars before coming to a stop. There's not a scratch on anything.

Minutes seem to pass, and I literally can't quit shaking as a car slowly inches past. The driver rolls down his window and says, "I'm in the Navy on leave. When I saw you coming up on me, I knew the rest of my leave was over. I don't know how you did it. Thanks." Someone, somewhere was helping steer my truck this evening.

When we return to Payson, Tyk tells us he's ready to move on. We're sad to see him leave, but I sense that it's time for a change. Running the FindMoreBuyers.com website for the past few years has allowed me to become very adept at internet marketing.

During one of my phone calls with Manas I mention that I'm thinking about selling the FindMoreBuyers.com website and ask him if he has any interest. The traffic that the website's generating is worth several thousands of dollars of sales every month.

Manas says he's interested, we agree on a price, and complete the transfer of the URL ownership.

Once we've sold the website, Lynne and I form a new company, and call it L&L Marketing, Inc. I've accumulated a few bucks, but I'm out of work once more. I'll soon be 65 years old and don't have a pension to fall back on. We can't live on Social Security alone, so I better find a way to generate some income.

It's time to embark on another adventure.

23 | Camelot

Now that John has his own home and we can live with a smaller office space, we feel like we're just bouncing around in our 3,000 square foot home. Real estate prices have gone up substantially since we bought our home and we decide to downsize. We put a big number on our home and try to sell it ourselves. It doesn't sell in a month, so we put up a sign offering to pay selling broker commissions.

Within a week, we receive an offer from a real estate broker from a couple offering a little less than we're asking. We accept the offer and still sell it for more than forty percent more than we paid for the home.

We quickly find a much smaller home at 1402 Sunset Drive, buy it and move in. It's about half the size of our previous home, on the side of a hill in a cul-de-sac. I immediately tear out an old pot-bellied stove, build-in a gas fireplace entertainment center and update the kitchen. The yard is unfenced, so we install fencing so our 4-legged family members can run around.

The only drawback to this home is having to climb a flight of stairs to get into the home from the garage level. However, the home is eminently livable and we quickly settle in.

After we've been in our new home for about six months, we start to miss the forever view of our previous home. Mollie has joined Buddy as four-legged members of our family and we take the kiddos on both morning and evening walks. As we're walking the dogs one morning, we see a realtor 'for sale' sign on an old Alpine style home that's been empty for years. The address is 1205 N Camelot Lane, and the front yard is so overgrown with brush, the house is barely visible.

Less than a month later, another realtors sign appears. We walk around the back of the house, up a rickety set of stairs to a deck that's sliding down the hill. My God, what a view! We find ourselves treated to an unobstructed 180-degree view of the entire Mogollon rim.

We call the realtor with the listing and schedule a walk through with him. This home was built by a Mid-West couple twenty-five or thirty years prior and the wife decided she didn't want to live in it. The home became a vacation rental and has been unoccupied the past 10 years. A local real estate investor just purchased it, marked it up and immediately put it back on the market.

To say that this home is in rough shape is definitely an understatement. But we see beyond the present existing problems and instead see lots of potential.

We try to picture how the home could be remodeled, and decide that the interior needs to be entirely gutted. The deck is sliding down the hill. The 10' by 10' kitchen is tiny and abominable. The main bath is dark and so small that both shoulders touch the walls when you sit on the toilet.

The home has heating strips under the windows and no air conditioning. The water heater and washer-dryer are located in the front entry. The carpeting was probably nice at one time.

However, the location is fantastic and the view is absolutely stunning. We decide to buy it.

We're comfortably living in our Sunset Drive home a half-mile away, so my job for the next six months is remodeling our new home. I quickly realize that at age 65, I'm going to need some help. Mike, one of my friends from church is a handyman/contractor and I ask him if he knows anyone that can help me. He says that he's using guys living in a half-way house in town and will have some of them with him the following morning.

He suggests we meet at a coffee shop in town at 8:00 a.m. and I can hire one of them if I want.

Mike is at the coffee shop when I arrive with three or four men in their early 30's from the halfway house. We have a cup of coffee and I describe the type of help I need and ask if anyone's interested. I tell them that I'll pay $10 per hour cash every day.

Gary Richards, one of the guys at the table, volunteers and we drive to our new home. Gary rides a bicycle to the house every day for weeks and we develop a close relationship.

I draw plans to convert the large existing 2-car garage into a master bedroom suite and build an addition, including a new garage, on the front of the house. We rip out walls and enlarge the existing kitchen. The water-heater and washer-dryer are relocated and we replace all the windows and doors.

The walls and ceilings of the entire home are finished with a rough sand finish that promises to scrape the skin off any knuckle that dares get too close. It takes an entire week and many carbide scrapers to remove the sand finish from the walls and ceilings. It's brutal work and I go through 4 or 5 temporary helpers in the process.

The home was originally built in a ginger-bread Alpine style, with a tall steep roof. The outside is sheathed in ugly blue vertical steel siding. All of that has to come off and we fill a couple of large roll-off dumpsters. The entire house needs to be re-wired. I hire Robert, a handyman electrician, to put in a new 200 ampere panel and we re-wire the home.

New maple cabinets are installed in the kitchen and baths. Jimi Harris is a master tile and stone mason and installs large Italian porcelain floor tile throughout the entire home along with travertine showers and kitchen backsplash. The entire back deck is removed and dragged, chunk by chunk, into the dumpsters.

The weeks turn into months and I hire many additional men from the halfway house. Typically, these are guys with a drug or alcohol problem, or who have just been released from prison. All told, I spend over $18,000 on halfway house help at $10 per hour.

After 6 solid months of 6-day a week effort, we have the final building inspection on the first phase of our remodeling project. Although our home's a long way from being finished, it's ready to move into.

There's still a 1,000 square foot unfinished walk-out basement with rough concrete block walls to be completed. The deck's been removed and now there's an eight-foot drop to the ground from the three sliding glass doors in the rear of the house.

However, the home's complete enough to be livable. We decide to list our home on Sunset Drive.

Property values are still frothy and homes are selling as soon as they hit the market. We decide to sell the home ourselves and I place a small ad in the real estate section of the Payson Roundup, our local town newspaper. We immediately have a bidding war on our home.

The second day the ad appears, we agree to sell our home to a couple moving into the area. The wife is a schoolteacher and the husband is a county employee.

The following day another couple comes by and offers us several thousand dollars more than we're asking.

However, we've given our word to the first couple and have to reject their offer. As it is, we've owned the home about a year and, thanks to the remodeling, are making a very nice profit.

We close escrow in under thirty days and move into our new home on Camelot Lane.

24 | Gary

Most people casually move through your life, sometimes leaving brief memories, and sometimes leaving semi-permanent tracks. A few people will leave permanent footprints on your heart. Gary Richards is one of the very few that become a permanent part of your life.

This is Gary's story, and it's become an integral part of my story.

When I meet Gary at the coffee shop, I have no idea what he's been through in his life. All I'm looking for is somebody that can help me remodel my home. I never expect that I'll be the person to help someone remodel his life.

Gary grows up in Kohl's Ranch, about 15 miles east of Payson. His father is addicted to heroin and dies when he's a teenager. His mother is an alcoholic and a waitress at the Christopher Creek Lodge. He never has an adult male as an example to model his life after.

Gary's living out of his car in the high school parking lot when he graduates from Payson high school. He falls into bad company and is soon arrested for kiting checks, leading to a five-year stint in prison. A tough kid, he's recruited by the older inmates to be their enforcer, leading to multiple run-ins with the prison guards and time in solitary.

Although he's never been involved with drugs, Gary's introduced to and becomes addicted to methamphetamine while in prison.

When he's released from prison, he starts selling and dealing drugs. He's recruited to be a drug driver, delivering drug shipments across the state. On one fateful trip, he's pulled over and arrested on drug charges. He's sentenced to an additional 8-year prison term, which leads to him spending an additional 6 years and 9 months in prison.

He's ultimately released from a correctional facility in Holbrook, Arizona. At the time, he has no money in his pocket, and is given a pair of women's shorts, a jacket and a pair of flip-flops for the 95 mile walk back to Payson. It's June, 2005,

He walks about 15 miles down State Hwy 377 on his way back to Payson when his flip-flops finally give out. Not knowing what to do, he starts praying for help.

Within minutes he sees a pair of shoes lying alongside the road. He puts them on and they're a perfect fit. His good fortune continues as he gets a lift from a passing motorist. After being dropped off in Heber, he walks until he hitches a ride for the final 50 miles to Payson.

Gary's on probation, specifically ordered to avoid drugs and is given a drug test by his probation officer on a frequent basis. He's out of work, living in a halfway house, without transportation. He's only been out of prison for a short time when Mike picks him up at the halfway house and we meet at the coffee shop.

Gary's smart, and a very hard worker. After working with him for a few days, I recognize that he has a genuinely good spirit and is committed to turning his life around. We develop a genuine friendship.

Shortly after Lynne and I move into our new home, we're able to create an area behind some trees in front of our house to park our travel trailer. Gary takes up temporary residence in the trailer, saving him the arduous bicycle ride up the hill to our home each day.

Now it's time to complete our home. The first thing on the list is to build a new deck to replace the one we tore down. The original deck had been built on six footings, none of which were more than a foot deep. In fact, when we bought the home, the deck was sliding down the hill on the second set of footings. The original footings are now located a couple of feet further down the hill. I'm determined that this new deck won't ever slide down the hill.

I rent a two-man gas powered posthole digger with a two-foot auger. We need to get at least six inches into undisturbed original soil to make sure the deck never moves again. Unfortunately, there's layer of heavy clay a foot or two below the surface of the ground and the auger won't cut it. Gary volunteers to dig the post holes by hand.

What a terrible job! Progress is made inches at a time and he pours sweat. After many hours, the deepest footing is finally over six feet deep, and the others aren't much shallower.

Once the forms are in place and footings complete, iron re-bar in place and concrete poured, we build a 750 square foot deck. It's topped with Trex decking. We want an unobstructed view of the forest below, so I build the outside railing using tempered sliding glass door panels.

The deck is awesome. We have an unobstructed 180-degree view, overlooking thousands of trees and the Mogollon Rim, some 20 miles away.

Gary's able to rent a small apartment and buy an old Honda Accord. His probation officer constantly checks up on Gary, and I get to know him on a casual basis. After Gary's been living in his own apartment for a short time, he makes a bad mistake. A friend comes by with drugs and talks Gary into using for the first time in years.

He's caught by the next pee test, his probation is violated, and he's sentenced to an additional three and a half years in prison. I'm devastated.

Gary is sentenced to serve his sentence at the prison in Buckeye, Arizona. While Gary's in prison, he becomes a fire-fighter and joins the prison hotshot crew. He travels with the fire crew throughout Arizona and works on his physical, mental and spiritual health.

We write letters back and forth constantly and I see that Gary's totally committed to turning his life around. We remain in constant communication, and I build a file containing dozens of his letters while he serves his time.

On December 8, 2008, Gary's released from prison, and I meet him outside the Buckeye prison gate. Gary has two brothers and a sister, all of whom are addicted to drugs and live in the area. He doesn't want to go back to the environment that's caused all of his problems, so I drive him to a halfway house in Prescott.

Lynne and I go to Safeway and stock up a bunch of groceries for him while he acclimates back into civilized society and finds a job. He doesn't know what to do and is scared for his future.

I tell Gary that he has a job. His job is to spend eight hours a day, five days a week, looking for work until someone hires him. This is a terrible time of the year to look for work. It's a couple of weeks before Christmas and the weather's bitterly cold.

He talks with dozens of businesses around Prescott and fills out over 20 job applications before he lands a job with a tree trimming company. Gary soon becomes adept climbing, trimming and removing trees.

After working for a couple of different employers, he lands a job with a national Class A construction company as a laborer. His honesty and work ethic are quickly recognized and he's given more and more responsibility. Gary obtains a Class C driver's license, soon becomes a foreman and valued company employee.

While running early one morning he meets Deanna and the sparks fly between them. Deanna's the mother of two beautiful young twin girls. They soon develop a relationship, become a married couple and Gary has a ready-made family.

Today he continues to make a positive difference in the lives of many people. I'm proud to remain his friend and mentor.

25 | RV Meetup.com

During Spring 2008, I attend a marketing seminar in Dallas put on by Scott Bolsch. He's one of the current internet marketing gurus making tens of thousands of dollars each month. About 100 people are in the room and I notice that I'm the oldest person here.

The focus of the seminar and much of the discussion relates to the value of niche marketing. As we love to travel, I register the domain 'RVMeetup.com' and decide to build a website targeting RV owners.

I intend to build a website that'll be an internet portal for RV owners. The website will provide full mapping capability and users will be able to plan trips and review all the RV parks along the way as they plan their route.

The website will also provide RVer's with the capability to stay in touch with other RVer's and post photos of their own adventures. Revenue will be generated by ads from RV parks along with additional revenue marketing other RV products and services on the website.

We've been using the heck out of our travel trailer and decide it's time to move up to a motor home. We visit a few RV dealers in the Phoenix area and purchase a 35-foot 2008 Fleetwood Southwind. We register the motorhome in the company name and it becomes a business asset.

We plaster 'RV Meetup.com' on the front and sides of the coach and take all the tax credits and deductions involved. All of our RV travel now becomes a tax-deductible expense.

We're excited about our new Class A Motorhome and take it out for a few short trips of a few days each around our local area. The thing that I appreciate most about our new rig is that it automatically levels itself with the push of a button. Unlike our old travel trailer, there's no longer a need to stack leveling blocks under the tires.

Lynne's favorite part is that she can use the bathroom while we're traveling. We tow our Hybrid Mercury Mariner, giving us full mobility at every place we stop.

In late June, 2009, we take the first long trip in our new rig. We visit the iconic national parks in Utah – Zion, Bryce, and Arches – spending a couple of days in each area, before heading north. After a few days in Grand Teton, we continue north for a week in Yellowstone National Park.

Although these National Parks are all awe inspiring, each in their own way, Glacier National Park is our favorite. We hike a couple miles and rest beside an ice-cold crystal-clear mountain lake surrounded by a half-dozen waterfalls feathering their way down the mountainsides from the glaciers above.

A few days later we're one of the lead cars to cross the Rocky Mountains on the 'Going-to-the-Sun' highway as it opens for the first day of the summer season. Huge piles of downed trees and rocks from winter avalanches line the road, and the snow is still over two feet deep at the top of the pass.

Days pass quickly, and sadly it's time to leave Glacier and get back on the road. We head east across the northern tier of the nation, spending a couple of days in every scenic park along the way until we make our way to Michigan.

After spending a full week with the family, we circle back to our home in Payson. By the time we get back home, we discover we've driven almost 5,000 miles. From an expense standpoint, our timing couldn't be much worse. The price of gas is at an all-time high and we fill up our 75-gallon gas tank many times with $4.00 per gallon gasoline. Our new rig only gets about 7 miles per gallon, so this ends up being a very pricey trip.

We're relieved to return home in late-August, having been on the road over 7 weeks.

Right after returning home, I receive a phone call from Daniel Taft, the owner of Computer Solutions, a local computer sales, service and repair company. I've used Daniel a number of times when I'm unable to fix the computer I've screwed up and need someone with more expertise than me. Daniel says he always hates to come to my home office because he knows it's going to be a lot more than a surface problem.

Daniel tells me that he's planning to build an RV site and wants to know if I can find a list of RV owners for him. I ask him for more information and he tells me it's for a client of his who registered some long, screwy website address and owes him money.

I tell Daniel that I own the website address of RVMeetup.com and ask him if he'd have an interest in a business arrangement using my URL. He's very receptive and we meet to work out the details.

Daniel agrees to take over the website development and I agree to take a minority equity position if he'll fund the operation. He talks with his own financial backer and agrees to put up enough money to get the project going.

He spends thousands of dollars with a website development company in India who takes his money but never delivers a product.

I ask him why he's using programmers in India and he tells me he did it because they work more cheaply than website developers in America. Given the lack of results he's been getting, I tell him that I think it's damn expensive.

Daniel spends thousands more with a designer for a spiffy logo for RVMeetup. After a few months, he loses interest in the project and the website is never completed. It's disappointing, but this unfinished adventure has provided us with significant financial and tax benefits.

The following year we embark on a 6-week RV trip exploring the western edge of America. We travel all the way up Highway 1 along the coast of the Pacific Ocean until we reach the Olympic National Park at the northernmost point in the United States.

Hwy 1 is a windy, tortuous road with at least 200 sharp curves with a maximum 15 mph speed. Some of the curves are so sharp the side of the motorhome often passes within 6 inches from the rock wall beside the road. When this happens, Lynne just closes her eyes. Both the trip and the Olympic forest are unforgettable.

And, from a tax perspective, it's been a real boon. Our accountant tells us we've received thousands of dollars of tax credits and write-offs as a result of our failed marketing effort. Plus, we get to deduct all of our fuel and travel expense while we travel the country.

Lynne and I have many adventures with this motorhome. We spend time in Ensenada, Mexico and drive across the Baja peninsula on 2-lane curvy mountain roads twenty feet wide, without a road shoulder. The Mexican 18-Wheelers coming toward us hug the center line and we pick up a few scratches on our rig from the brush on the side of the road. Both our butt-cheeks are squeezed tight, and sometimes we go 20 minutes without either of us saying a word.

We park the rig on the beach in San Felipe, Mexico and watch the tide move in and out, exposing a half mile of sea floor.

The part we enjoy most is that we're able to have all of these adventures and sleep in the same bed every night.

RVMeetup.com allows us to travel throughout the Western United States and spend time exploring 8 of the 10 most popular National Parks in America with pre-tax dollars.

The memories we make are priceless. It doesn't get any better than this.

26 | L&L Marketing

I've taken the last six months away from my business to turn a sow's ear into our dream home. The only thing yet to be completed is to turn our unfinished walk-out basement into a finished entertainment room.

I expect to complete the downstairs project in the spare time I always imagine I have, but never quite seem to find. Now it's time to get back to work and generate some income.

I take a chance that my business experience and knowledge of internet marketing is broad enough to allow me to move into the affiliate marketing arena.

Affiliate marketing is essentially buying ads on various search engines and websites to advertise the products and services of other companies. I only make money when somebody clicks on my ad and buys the item that I'm advertising. It's as easy to lose big money as it is to make big money.

Actually, it's probably easier to lose money. Only, not 'probably'. I estimate that I spend about $10,000 more than we bring in that first year while I'm learning what not to do. Undeterred, I keep pushing ahead.

I soon learn that if you can't accurately measure the precise results obtained by every ad you buy on every page of every website on which that ad is placed for every keyword you bid on, you'll surely spend more money than you make. The key is to find out what works and do more of it. Even more important is to learn what's not working and stop spending money there.

I finally find a software tool that will do exactly what I need, and I'm off to the races. My years of experience in so many different areas give me an advantage, even though I'm competing with internet marketers less than half my age.

I learn that there's both a blessing and a curse involved with this new business. The down side is that it's very time consuming. It must be attended to every day if I want to continue to generate a profit. It takes me 10 or more hours daily to keep bids at the top of the search engines.

The up side is we're soon making a substantial five-figure income almost every month.

For several years, whether vacationing in Mexico, or travelling around the country in our motorhome, I find myself spending 4 to 6 hours every day on the business. Because everything is done online, I can work from literally anywhere in the world I can get an internet connection. I've learned that if I can keep up the business on a daily basis, we continue to make good money. A week of inactivity, and our profits go through the floor.

While all of this is going on, it's time to complete our dream home. The downstairs unfinished walkout basement comes to the top of my to-do list. The 1,000 square foot room becomes an entertainment mecca with a large built-in entertainment center, wet bar and half bath. The bumper-pool table, tournament dart board and hobby room complete the project.

As a friend once commented, "every square inch is decorated". Camelot is now our complete dream home.

Out of the blue an old part of my life resurfaces. Terry Allen calls and says he wants to meet me. He's trying to publish a book focusing solely on the words of Jesus. This is the third time he's come into my life and his project sounds positive.

Perhaps, with the passage of time, he's learned to practice what he preaches. I agree to meet with him.

He wants to legally change his last name to 'Christian', so I file the papers for him. When Terry asks me to participate in a new venture to publish his book, I agree and spend a fair amount of time and money helping him with his project.

Unfortunately, once I spend time with him, I find that he hasn't changed. He's still bad news. I wash my hands of him and wish him Godspeed.

I'm now in my early 70's, making more money than I've ever made in my life. I decide that I need someone to help me in the business. Lori, my youngest daughter, is a stay-at-home mom and I'm able to enlist her to help me manage the bidding process. She participates in the profit that we generate and the business continues to prosper.

In 2011 I decide that Lori and I ought to attend the annual *ad:tech* conference in San Francisco. There are hundreds of vendors and over two thousand attendees swarming Moscone Center in San Francisco. We spend three days at the conference and I discover that I'm the oldest person there. We make some new contacts and have a great time enjoying the fare in the San Francisco Chinatown.

I've found a combination of offers – primarily auto insurance and income tax preparation – and advertising methods that are extremely lucrative. However, my competition as an advertiser has been getting much stiffer, almost on a monthly basis.

So, I decide to travel to a 2-day internet marketing seminar in San Diego in the summer of 2013. The marketing material for the seminar promises to teach a brand-new internet marketing technique that will create thousands of dollars of profit.

The seminar entrance fee is $2,000. I hope to pick up something that I can use to make my daily grind a little easier. It's a big gathering and there are probably 250 internet marketers and wannabe marketers in attendance. I look around and see that I'm the oldest person here, too.

You can't believe my astonishment and dismay when the first half of the first day of the seminar, the presenter teaches everybody exactly what I've been doing for the past several years. I can't believe it! I know that'll absolutely kill my business, and it does. The price for the ads that I've been running soon triples. Within a matter of weeks, my business is no longer profitable.

I'm tired of years of competing, ready to enjoy life, and decide it's time to hang up my internet marketing cleats for good.

However, life isn't through with me yet. I'm still in excellent health and have another chapter or two yet to write.

27 | John

A memorable line in an old movie goes, "Life is like a box of chocolates. You never know what you're going to get". The implication is that no matter what you pick out of the box, it's all good. Maybe, just what you didn't expect. Lynne's son John is like one of those chocolates. He's sweet and an unexpected treasure.

John was in a terrible auto accident when he was 18 years old. Riding in the back seat of a Camaro, because of alcohol and excess speed, the driver isn't able to navigate a turn and the car hits a house. The only one in the car that's seriously injured is John. His head slams into the doorpost and he suffers a traumatic brain injury, spending many weeks at the University of Michigan Hospital in a coma.

He slowly begins to regain consciousness after six weeks and isn't expected to be able to ever walk or talk again. However, John fools everybody.

Fortunately, the accident happens in Michigan, a state with no-fault insurance laws. Lynne is insured by AAA Michigan and under the no-fault law, AAA is responsible for all of the expenses caused by the accident, including full medical care. Costs quickly rise into the millions of dollars, and all of John's accident related expenses are fully covered.

John receives months and years of continuous treatment and physical therapy, but the left side of his body remains partially paralyzed. Although his short term memory is badly compromised, John is walking and talking. He receives the best, cutting-edge medical care, but nothing that modern medicine can provide is able to return his body to normal.

He has every right to be resentful for the hand that life has dealt him, but his attitude remains upbeat and cheerful. One evening after dinner we're talking about John's disability and John says, "After the accident they said I was going to be a vegetable. Do I look like a carrot?".

I crack-up at his sense of humor and learn to appreciate and love John just as he is.

John enters into a short-term marriage in Michigan in spite of our misgivings and warnings and becomes the biological father to two sons. The marriage doesn't last and soon ends.

Lynne has been his caretaker since his accident so when we move to Arizona, John comes along as part of our family. Finding a place that will accommodate John's needs is paramount in finding the right home.

John continues physical therapy two days a week on an ongoing schedule and is extremely fortunate to find a physical therapist who takes it upon herself to make John's life as comfortable as possible. His brain injury has turned all of the muscles on the entire left side of his body into taut rubber bands and he receives weekly massages to keep his muscles pliable.

In spite of the physical pain and the many difficulties he experiences on a daily basis, John has a great sense of humor and laughs often. His favorite saying, and the one everybody knows him by is, "It doesn't get any better than this". John is mobile, and rides around Payson in a fancy recumbent 3-wheel cycle.

After sharing our home for 6 or 7 years, we get him his own place. He's grateful for the opportunity to live in his own home and remains semi-independent for 10 years.

He meets Melody, a young developmentally challenged woman, and they want to become husband and wife. We plan a beautiful wedding for John and Melody at a local Payson venue and dozens of friends and family are in attendance.

We don't want the responsibility of taking care of Melody should something happen to her mother, so don't file the marriage certificate.

Melody moves in with John and soon they join us on a week's Caribbean cruise. They both have a boisterous, happy time and their spontaneous laughter is contagious.

Unfortunately, after trying to live together for a few years, it just doesn't work out. They soon separate, but remain close friends and continue to speak daily on the phone.

After a few years, John exchanges his recumbent for an easier-to-ride trike and gets a job at an antique store. He develops a deep friendship with Don, the owner of the store. Don is in his 80's and they spend many hours keeping each other company.

I quickly learn that Johns favorite repair materials are duct tape and bungee cords. If it can't be fixed with one of those methods, it stays broken. I soon become his surrogate 'dad' and all-around fix-it man.

John is an integral part of our family and joins us on a number of our adventures. The week he spends with us in Hawaii is particularly memorable and we all have a wonderful time together.

Although we've all now lived in Arizona for 18 years, Lynne is missing her family. All of her children except John still live in Michigan, and she's the proud grandmother of 10 grandsons. They're marrying and starting families of their own and she wants to spend some time with them before they all fly away.

Amazingly, the home next door to Kristin, Lynne's daughter is listed for sale. After the original buyer backs out, late in 2014 we buy the home for John. That way, he'll have someone to look after him while he spends the summers in Michigan.

John's new home is actually old. It was built in 1941 and will need extensive remodeling, but it provides the foundation for things to come. John is again a home owner.

I'm not willing to spend 5-month long winters in Michigan, so we decide to sell our dream home and look for a home in the greater Tucson area. That way we'll be able to spend the winters in Arizona and the summers in Michigan.

In January 2015 we sell our Payson home at a substantial profit. Lynne and I move into John's small home for a couple of months while we look for a home large enough that we can all live in together.

After two months, we close escrow on a home that provides the space we need. It's not perfect, but

John has his own suite on one end of the home with a private bedroom, den and bath.

Once more it's time to embark on another adventure.

28 | The Remodeler

Real estate values hit their nadir in Spring 2012. Lots of people are upside down in their home and are finding that they owe the bank tens of thousands of dollars more than their home is worth.

Lynne's son Dan is one of those people. He discovers that his home is not only worth a whole lot less than his mortgage, but the swimming pool in the backyard has developed structural cracks and will cost thousands of dollars to repair.

If that's not bad enough, his marriage is disintegrating. His wife made some bad financial decisions, and as a consequence, his credit is in the dumpster. Dan separates from his wife and decides to let his home go into foreclosure. However, he still needs a place to live.

We tell him that if he can find a super good deal on a house that he wants to live in, we'll buy it and lease it back to him with an option to buy. Dan looks at homes in foreclosure and finds a home at 9733 Roosevelt St, in Taylor, Michigan. It's rough, but has a lot of potential.

We buy the home and Dan starts to remodel it. He tears out the kitchen and removes a big eyesore in the form of a broken-down above ground swimming pool. Then his life changes.

While he's in the midst of a nasty divorce, he meets and becomes engaged to Beth, who lives 35 miles away in St Clair Shores. Now that Dan has found mutual love, there's no reason for him to go back to his Taylor home. The remodel screeches to a halt and our house sits empty for over a year.

It's now Fall 2014, and Lynne is looking forward to spending summers in Michigan with her family. We drive back to Michigan and camp out in the Taylor home for a couple of weeks. The house has no kitchen, so we fill a couple of ice chests and use a camp stove for cooking.

We buy new cabinets and make arrangements with Lynne's nephew, a carpenter, to install the cabinets and replace a bunch of doors while we're in Arizona. He's extremely conscientious and does a great job.

Meanwhile, I'm having a problem with my feet going to sleep whenever I go hiking or stand in one spot for more than a few minutes. An MRI discloses the problem. My L4 vertebra has slid forward and the spinal cord is badly pinched. The MRI shows spinal fluid is totally cut off from the bottom of my spine.

The neurologist tells me that if I don't have spinal surgery pretty soon, I'll first lose bladder control and shortly thereafter be unable to walk. So, in addition to selling a home, buying a home and packing and moving, I need to schedule and recover from surgery.

It's going to be a fire drill.

We list and sell our Payson dream home and make a nice profit. We find and purchase a home in the Oro Valley, just north of Tucson. The home is completely original and terribly dated. We don't like the fact that when we look out the back window, we see directly into the kitchen of the home behind us.

Although it's badly dated, it has a layout that'll allow John to remain with us. If we're going to be happy here, it's going to need a complete remodel.

I schedule back surgery and we make arrangements with the movers. Looking at the calendar, we wonder how the hell we're going to get it all done.

We pack up all of our belongings, dividing everything into three piles.

One pile for John's stuff that's going to his new Michigan home.

Another pile of our stuff to take to Michigan.

The third pile of our belongings is going to our new Oro Valley home.

It's a nightmare trying to pack our 3,000 square foot home, having to determine the final destination of literally everything we own. A storage unit holds all of the items we'll be taking to Michigan.

Early in the morning on Valentine's day, Saturday, February 14, the movers empty our dream home and we all travel the four hours to Oro Valley. As soon as the truck's unloaded, I work like a banshee through Sunday trying to unpack all of our essential belongings.

I must, because I have back surgery scheduled at 11 a.m. the following day. I sure won't be any help for a few weeks. After 24 hours in the hospital, I get back home, unable to do more than sleep, eat and go to the bathroom.

It's been an absolutely frantic 72 hours.

As soon as I'm able to move around without too much discomfort, we start planning another major remodel. The home we purchased needs a complete make-over and we draw up remodeling plans. I interview a couple of general contractors and select one I feel I can trust to do the remodel while we spend the summer in Michigan. We'll be tearing out walls, replacing floors, putting in two new baths and switching the kitchen completely around.

We spend the next few weeks selecting new kitchen cabinets, bathroom vanities and fixtures, appliances, flooring, paint colors and the million and one things that go into a complete home remodel.

Our contractor, John Raymond, Sr., assures us he can have all of the work completed by the time we return in the fall. I've never attempted a remodel when I couldn't be there to personally supervise the job, and hope we are making the right decision.

After ten weeks of healing, I rent a moving truck, empty the storage unit and we make the 2,000 mile trek to Michigan without incident. We get John settled into his new home and Lynne and I move into the home we bought for Dan.

We now have a new, beautiful kitchen, but there are a zillion things to do to complete the remodel. I spend the entire summer working on the house and it becomes one of the nicest in the neighborhood. The biggest drawback is the location. Several times each week Lynne has to drive 30 to 40 minutes each way to take care of John's needs.

Speaking of John, his home is badly in need of help. Although the kitchen is virtually unusable, John makes it work through the summer. We make arrangements with Armand, a former son-in-law, to remodel the kitchen and clean up the upstairs over the winter months. I design a new layout for the tiny kitchen and we pick out the cabinets, appliances and flooring. Everything's ready for Armand to complete the work while snow is on the ground.

During that summer I fly back to Arizona to supervise the cabinet installation and review the progress on our remodel. Within a week, the cabinets, appliances and countertops are installed. What a difference this remodel is making! With a new interior layout, it barely looks like the same home we bought.

We return to Oro Valley in the fall. Our basic home remodel is complete, but lots of details remain. Soon the backsplash is installed, the boxes unpacked and we find time to relax. I build a feature wall with a fireplace and floating shelves in the Great Room and our home is featured in the annual community home tour.

John settles into his 'private suite' and spends many enjoyable hours each week working with clay and playing bocce ball. Life quiets down and the winter months quickly pass.

The following Spring 2016, we all return to Michigan. Armand has turned John's almost 70-year old home into a most livable place. Again, the biggest challenge is the distance between our home in Taylor and John's home in Berkley. We start looking for a small home Lynne and I can spend summers in that'll be close to John's home.

We look at new real estate listings online every morning. After several weeks of serious looking, we find an 1,100 square foot home in Troy, only two and a half miles away from John.

We attempt to buy the home, only to find that someone beat us to the punch and the home owner has already accepted an offer. We're bummed, but keep searching. About a month later, we see that the same home is again listed for sale online. We learn that the buyer wasn't able to qualify for a loan, so we quickly make an all-cash offer and it becomes ours.

Again, we just bought a home that needs a lot of work.

The previous owner was a smoker and the walls all have to be sealed with lacquer to kill the tobacco odor. The old flooring is removed, and we discover six different layers and types of flooring on top of each other in a couple of rooms.

The tiny three-bedroom house is soon converted to a two-bedroom home with a large master bedroom suite. I again hire Armand to help with the remodel and drive 30 miles each way from our home in Taylor for a couple of months as we make the home livable.

Fortunately, we're able to stay in our Taylor home while all the work is going on. As the remodel is nearing completion, we list our home in Taylor for sale and soon have another bidding war going on.

This former foreclosure property has become one of the most desirable homes in the neighborhood. As it turns out, the home appraises for slightly less than the offer we accept, but we're very pleased and make another nice profit.

It looks like this is becoming a habit. Once again, we've turned a sow's ear into a silk purse.

After two months of steady work, we settle into our newly remodeled home in Troy. We love our home and the final months of summer quickly pass. John enjoys being able to live next door to his sister and we anticipate having more time with the family. However, the days start getting shorter and nights are getting colder. We close up the house and hit the road again, looking forward to spending the winter months back in Oro Valley.

Shortly before the Christmas holiday season we get together with Ted and Judy, friends living about a block down on the other side of the street, for a glass of wine. Their home is about 500 square feet smaller than ours and backs up to a natural area of State-owned property. The home has a huge back yard with an unobstructed view of the mountains. Million-dollar homes sit on a ridge on the other side of a natural wash.

Although it's only a block away, the property location is absolutely stunning.

Everything in their home is original. Nothing has been touched since it was built over 25 years ago. To our surprise, Ted and Judy tell us that they're going to sell their home. They want to move back to Colorado to be closer to their kids. Lynne and I look at each other and know what we have to do.

I ask Ted how much they want for their home. When Ted gives me a number, I tell him we'll give him what he's looking for, and do it without getting a realtor involved. We shake hands and start making a list of all the things the home needs.

I draw up plans to add a mother-in-law suite in the back of the home for John. The kitchen needs to be totally gutted and walls removed to bring everything up to date.

It looks like we have one more remodel to look forward to. We close escrow and the home becomes ours.

We interview a couple of real estate agents and soon list our newly remodeled home for sale. We receive a several offers, and after a couple of hiccups, find a cash buyer. Once again, our home sale produces a nice profit.

As soon as Ted and Judy move out, I update the bedrooms and master bath so we have a place to live. I hire the same contractor that remodeled the home we just sold, trusting him to do as good a job on this new home. Lynne, John and I soon move and settle in for the balance of the winter months.

However, things have a way of working out in ways that you can't foresee. Lynne and I are now in our mid-70's and she's known that there was going to be a time when she'd no longer be able to care for John's needs. She's been his caretaker and responsible for his well-being ever since his auto accident occurred over 35 years ago.

John still has close friends living in Payson and Lynne drives him up for a visit. On the way back to Oro Valley, she suddenly realizes that the day has arrived to turn John's care over to somebody else. She's had discussions with her daughter, Kristin, about taking over as John's caretaker when that time comes.

That time is now. We scrap plans to build the mother-in-law addition and Kristin makes plans to take care of John's needs.

The temperature in Arizona is rising, and soon it's time to head back to Michigan for the summer months. I rent a small U-Haul trailer and load John's electric scooter and all of his personal stuff. He'll now be a permanent resident in Michigan.

Lynne and I move back to our cute home in Troy for the summer. However, the dreams of lots of weekend get-togethers with the family don't materialize. It seems that everybody is so busy with their lives that spending time with the grandparents is at the end of their to-do list.

We decide now that Kristin is taking care of John, the expense and effort entailed in maintaining two homes is no longer worth it.

We list our Troy home for sale. Within 10 days we receive 5 full-price purchase offers. Our primary stipulation is that we can't close escrow until after we return from a 2-week trip to Rome including a 10-day cruise. We accept an offer that's specifically tailored to our needs. We've owned this home for one month longer than needed to qualify for long-term capital gains tax treatment and again make a nice profit.

We schedule an estate sale and drive back to Arizona with everything we plan to keep.

When we return, we discover that the contractor we hired has retired and the business is now being run by his son who is at best a rough carpenter. Our remodel is way behind schedule and we stay in a VRBO for a month.

This is the worst remodeling experience we've ever had. The contractor's son does a very poor job and I spend many months correcting and repairing the deficiencies we discover. In the long run, it doesn't matter. Our home is absolutely perfect and the last one we hope to live in.

Now, for the first time in 25 years, Lynne and I are a couple, rather than a family.

We've remodeled 5 different homes over the past 5 years, all while we're in our 70's. We're both in good health and enjoying every day. I promise Lynne that this is the last remodel.

Life is indeed good.

29 | How to Win in Life

Always....

Do the best you can,

with what you have,

where you are.

30 | Pre-Requiem

Putting my personal life story down in writing has been an eye-opening, occasionally mind-bending experience. Although this lifetime has provided the opportunity to experience many things, my only regret is that I've never been able to stick with any one thing long enough to be the very best at any single endeavor. Regardless, it's my journey.

Life has taught me that the destination's the same for all of us. Nobody gets out of here alive. Everything we experience is our own journey. That's all we have. A journey.

You produce the story of your own life journey. You're the writer, the director and the main character. You're also your own worst critic. Your journey is all about the choices you make. If you don't like the direction you're going, choose to change directions.

If you're not enjoying your journey now, when the hell do you plan to start?

Acknowledgments

This book could never have been written without the stability that my wife, Lynne Brophy, has brought into my life. Our backgrounds couldn't be more different, yet she has brought sorely missing balance into my life. My impulsiveness and spontaneity have been tempered by her even-keeled, mid-western demeanor and her constant love and support.

We are yin and yang.

I acknowledge the difficulties she's endured in being a life partner of someone with ADHD. I'm eternally grateful she stuck with me through the many challenging times we've experienced as husband and wife, especially as most were of my own creation.

Together, we've become an awesome team.

Many others have contributed to making this story possible. Some have been an example to live up to and others an example to avoid. I acknowledge their presence in my life and although they shall go unnamed, I'm grateful for the lessons they have taught.

Made in the USA
Columbia, SC
17 August 2020

16179407R00114